Especially for:

....

From:

....

Date:

....

When
Jesus
Speaks
to a
COURAGEOUS
Girl's
Heart

Published by Barbour Publishing, Inc., 1810 Barbour Drive, Uhrichsville, Ohio 44683, www.barbourbooks.com

Our mission is to inspire the world with the life-changing message of the Bible.

ecpa
Member of the
Evangelical Christian
Publishers Association

Printed in the United States of America.

000648 0221 BP

When Jesus Speaks to a

COURAGEOUS Girl's Heart

A Devotional

Janice Thompson

BARBOUR **kidz**

A Division of Barbour Publishing

Introduction

Did you realize that Jesus speaks to you every day? It's true! If you're listening closely, you'll hear His still, small voice. Shh! Can you hear Him? He's right there, whispering in your ear, telling you how special you are to Him and how He created you for amazing things. He's whispering, "You're destined for greatness, girl!"

Maybe you don't feel like you're destined for big things. Perhaps you're scared of what the future holds. Your knees are knocking, and your hands are shaking. Turn the pages of this book and watch as Jesus helps you grow bolder in your faith. These daily readings will encourage you to step out and do great things for Him, scared or not.

Through these devotions, you'll find wisdom you need to face the day, along with lovely little reminders that Jesus has a very special message just for you. You'll learn that He speaks courage into your heart—every day and in every situation—whether you're experiencing hurt, loneliness, anger, sadness, or joy. Each devotional, rooted in scripture and written from Christ's heavenly perspective, will leave you feeling perfectly loved and blessed.

C.O.U.R.A.G.E.

Psst! You! Yes, you! Lean in close. I've got something to tell you, something that might surprise you. Of all the girls on the planet, you're one of a kind. There's absolutely, positively no one like you. You can search far and wide, but you won't find a single soul who has your looks, your personality, and your amazing talents.

I made you one of a kind for a reason. You are uniquely you. . .on purpose. I plan to do amazing things through you, things that no one else can do. Oh, the places you'll go, kiddo! But before I do, I want to zap you with a little courage so that you're ready.

Let's break it down:

> C: Say the word *can* instead of *can't*. You can do it, kiddo!
>
> O: Obstacle. No obstacle is too big for Me. Trust Me to help you past it.
>
> U: Unique. I've made you to be unique, one of a kind.
>
> R: Righteous. Even when you mess up, you don't have to worry. It's My righteousness that matters.

A: Apple. You're the apple of My eye. I would do anything for you!

G: Greatness. That's your destiny!

E: Eternity. I've set your course from now until eternity. Once you're My child, you'll never have to worry about who's in control. I've got you—today, tomorrow, and forever. That should get you really, really excited!

"Be strong and have strength of heart. Do not be afraid or shake with fear because of them. For the Lord your God is the One Who goes with you. He will be faithful to you. He will not leave you alone." Then Moses called Joshua and said to him in front of all Israel, "Be strong and have strength of heart. For you will go with this people into the land the Lord has promised to their fathers to give them. And you will bring them in to take it. The Lord is the One Who goes before you. He will be with you. He will be faithful to you and will not leave you alone. Do not be afraid or troubled."

DEUTERONOMY 31:6–8

Things That Go Bump in the Night

I made you, so I know you inside and out. Sometimes you get scared. Everyone does, even grown-ups. When it happens, your knees knock. Your hands tremble. You feel like you can't breathe. Your courage flies away like a puff of smoke. *Poof!*

Here's a fun fact, one I hope you never forget: I didn't give you a spirit of fear. That means, I don't want you to be afraid. But there is someone who *does* want to scare you, and he's tricky! Some people call him the devil. Other people call him Satan. I call him the enemy! He's always trying to hurt My kids, and I'm over it! He needs to back off and leave My people alone!

If you're worried and fearful, you can say, "Get away from me, devil! I have power in Jesus' name!" It's true! When you speak My name, he has to run away. (That's a promise by the way, and I'm serious. Just speak My name, and Satan has to flee!)

No matter how scared you get, just come rushing to Me. Nothing you face is bigger than

Me. I'm your protector and your defender. I have given you a spirit of power and love and a sound mind. That means with My help, you're bigger and tougher than any boogie man! My Spirit lives inside of you and (wow!) are you ever powerful. So no more fear, girlie. Together we're a force for good!

♡ ♥ ♥ ♡ ♥ ♥

But now the Lord Who made you,
O Jacob, and He Who made you, O Israel,
says, "Do not be afraid. For I have bought
you and made you free. I have called you by
name. You are Mine! When you pass through
the waters, I will be with you. When you pass
through the rivers, they will not flow over you.
When you walk through the fire, you will not
be burned. The fire will not destroy you. For I
am the Lord your God, the Holy One of Israel,
Who saves you. I have given Egypt as pay for
your life, and have traded Cush and Seba for
you. You are of great worth in My eyes.
You are honored and I love you."
ISAIAH 43:1–4

Telling the Real Truth

Lots of people say that there are many roads to heaven. (Trust Me, I've heard all of their stories!) Some people think if you're a good person you'll get there because of your good works. Other people say it doesn't matter how you live your life or what you believe, everyone gets to go to heaven when they die. Some people even believe that all the religions of the world are pretty much the same and that all of them lead to Me. (Boy, are they way off!)

You know Me, sweet girl. I have to tell the truth. So, I'm here to tell you that there's really only *one* way to get to heaven. Yep, just one. And it's through Me. In order to get to heaven after you die, you have to first accept Me as Lord and Savior of your life. You have to say, "Jesus, come and live in my heart. Forgive me of my sins. Please be my Savior and my King!" When you do that, you've got a one-way ticket to eternal life with Me. And it's a ticket you can never tear up or throw away!

The next time someone tells you there are

many ways to get to heaven, work up the courage to speak the truth. It might be hard, but tell them about Me and how I came to save them. Then pray for that person to come to know Me like you do.

"Do not let your heart be troubled. You have put your trust in God, put your trust in Me also. There are many rooms in My Father's house. If it were not so, I would have told you. I am going away to make a place for you. After I go and make a place for you, I will come back and take you with Me. Then you may be where I am. You know where I am going and you know how to get there." Thomas said to Jesus, "Lord, we do not know where You are going. How can we know the way to get there?" Jesus said, "I am the Way and the Truth and the Life. No one can go to the Father except by Me. If you had known Me, you would know My Father also. From now on you know Him and have seen Him."

John 14:1–7

Call on Me

You are My precious child, and I see when you're in trouble. I hear you crying, "Help!" and I come running. I don't ever want you to feel alone. You're not. I'm always nearby, ready to lend a hand. (Can I be honest and tell you that it breaks My heart a little whenever you forget this? It really does!)

You've got wonderful people in your life. I know, because I put them there. Parents, grandparents, aunts, uncles, teachers, and friends. All of these people adore you too, and you can call on them when you're in trouble. In fact, I'm hoping you do! Some of them have lived a l-o-n-g time and have lots of wisdom. They will give awesome advice when you need it. But don't ever forget to invite Me to help. When you're in a real jam, just say, "Jesus, help!" and *vroom!* I'll show.up in a hurry, ready to get to work.

I'm your safe place, sweet girl. You can trust Me when I say I'm on your side. I've got your back, no matter what you're going through. So when you're feeling sad or when you're hurting, just come to Me. My ears are wide open, and I love to hear about all the things you're going through. I'm your helper and your friend.

God is our safe place and our strength. He is always our help when we are in trouble. So we will not be afraid, even if the earth is shaken and the mountains fall into the center of the sea, and even if its waters go wild with storm and the mountains shake with its action. There is a river whose waters make glad the city of God, the holy place where the Most High lives. God is in the center of her. She will not be moved. God will help her when the morning comes. The people made noise. The nations fell. He raised His voice and the earth melted. The Lord of All is with us. The God of Jacob is our strong place.
PSALM 46:1–7

My Story

Hey, sweet girl! I want to tell you a story about something that happened to Me a long time ago. Maybe you've already heard that I came from heaven down to earth and was born as a baby. My mother was named Mary. She was an amazing mom. I also loved hanging out with My earthly dad, Joseph. He taught Me how to be a carpenter, just like him. I had a pretty normal life, I guess you could say.

When I grew up, the time came to show the world who I *really* was—the Son of God and the Savior of the world. I knew it would be an adventure, and I could hardly wait to get started! I gathered a team of friends around Me, and we started sharing the good news about how much God loves people. This message came as a surprise to many, because they always thought God was far off, way out of reach. They didn't see Him as the loving type.

Not everyone liked the message I was spreading. Some people didn't believe Me. Other people thought I was making up the story about being God's Son. They got so angry that they decided to abuse Me and then kill Me.

Don't worry, though! My story has a good ending. I rose from the dead and proved once and for all that I'm really, truly the Savior of the world. So when you tell people about Me, don't forget to tell them the part about how I came back to life. It's all the proof you'll need that I'm really God's Son.

The people were looking for something to happen. They were thinking in their hearts about John the Baptist. They wondered if he might be the Christ. But John said to all of them, "I baptize you with water. There is One coming Who is greater than I. I am not good enough to get down and help Him take off His shoes. He will baptize you with the Holy Spirit and with fire. He comes ready to clean the grain. He will gather the grain and clean it all. He will put the clean grain into a building. But He will burn that which is no good with a fire that cannot be put out."
LUKE 3:15–17

The Courage to Be Yourself

Sweet girl, I saw what happened in the lunch room that day. I know how mean the other girls were to you, how they left you out and then made fun of you. I saw your broken heart, and My heart broke too. I wish those girls would shape up, but right now it doesn't look like they want to.

Here's a hard truth: you won't always fit into every circle. And think about it from My point of view. I created you with your own unique fingerprint, your own DNA, and your own personality. And all of those girls around you? They're working too hard to be like everyone else. If they really took the time to slow down and read My Word, they would see that I created them to be unique too. They wouldn't worry so much about fitting in.

It's going to take courage to be yourself. Don't waste too much time worrying about fitting into this group or that group. And please don't fret over the things in your life that aren't perfect now. Because I created you to be your own true self, I've got plans in mind just for you.

I know where you're headed, who your friends will be, and all of the amazing things you're going to accomplish. Hang in there, kiddo! You do you, boo!

Samuel said, "I have come in peace to give a gift to the Lord. Make yourselves holy and come with me as I give the gift." He set apart Jesse and his sons also, and asked them to come to the gift-giving. When they had come, Samuel looked at Eliab and thought, "For sure he is the Lord's chosen one who is standing before Him." But the Lord said to Samuel, "Do not look at the way he looks on the outside or how tall he is, because I have not chosen him. For the Lord does not look at the things man looks at. A man looks at the outside of a person, but the Lord looks at the heart."

1 SAMUEL 16:5–7

The Belly of the Whale

I see what's going on in that head of yours, girlie. You wish you could just run away from your problems and forget about them.

I don't really blame you. Life is hard. You're getting fed up and tired of facing those pesky problems. You wish you could just pack up your bags and move to a tropical island, away from all the people who bug you. (That does sound like fun, doesn't it?) Maybe if you did, all of your irritating struggles would go away. (Hint: they won't!)

You might remember a Bible story about a guy name Jonah who did try to run away. I asked him to do something hard and he didn't want to, so he ran. Boy, did he run! He boarded a ship, got tossed overboard, and ended up in the belly of a whale. Now, I'm not saying you'll end up in a fish's tummy if you get scared and run, but it's always safer to do the right thing, even if it's hard. And trust Me when I say that I'll get you through those problems, no matter how tough they seem. It's always better to learn your lessons than to run away.

I was gracious to Jonah. He lived to tell his story. I'm really good at giving second chances. I'll be gracious to you too. But I still hope you'll stay put and learn your lessons.

The Lord sent a big fish to swallow Jonah, and he was in the stomach of the fish for three days and three nights. Then Jonah prayed to the Lord his God while in the stomach of the fish, saying, "I called out to the Lord because of my trouble, and He answered me. I cried for help from the place of the dead, and You heard my voice. You threw me into the deep waters, to the very bottom of the sea. A flood was all around me and all Your waves passed over me. Then I said, 'I have been sent away from Your eyes. But I will look again toward Your holy house.' Waters closed in over me. The sea was all around me. Weeds were around my head. I went down to the roots of the mountains. The walls of the earth were around me forever. But You have brought me up from the grave, O Lord my God. While I was losing all my strength, I remembered the Lord. And my prayer came to You, into Your holy house."
JONAH 1:17–2:7

The Sin Pit

Some of your friends are a little on the naughty side, aren't they? It seems like they're always in trouble—with their parents, their teachers, even some of the neighbors. Those not-so-nice kids think no one sees what they're up to, but I see. I can even see into their imaginations to know what crazy plots they're dreaming up next. And I'm here to tell you. . .it's not good. They love hanging out in the sin pit. Their actions are all the proof you need that they're headed down the wrong road.

Here's a suggestion: you might need to step away from those troublemakers, at least for now. Especially the ones who are doing bad things on purpose. (Hey, it's one thing to slip up and do something bad. But when you plan it in advance? Well, that takes it to a whole new level!)

When they come up with their plans to hurt others, they're really hurting themselves. . .and Me. It breaks My heart to see any of My kids doing bad things. Oh, how I wish they would stop living like that!

I want you to make good plans and do good things with your life. Don't fall—*splat!*—into the naughty pit. Live a holy life, one you can be proud of. I want the very best for you, you know! It takes loads of courage to live a holy life, but with My help, you can do it!

God is always right in how He judges.
He is angry with the sinful every day. If a
man is not sorry for his sins and will not turn
from them, God will make His sword sharp.
He will string His bow and make it ready.
He takes up His sword and the bow of death.
And He makes arrows of fire. See how the
sinful man thinks up sins and plans trouble and
lies start growing inside him. He has dug out a
deep hole, and has fallen into the hole he has
dug. The trouble he makes will return to him.
When he hurts others it will come down on
his own head. I will give thanks to the Lord
because He is right and good. I will sing praise
to the name of the Lord Most High.
PSALM 7:11–17

Power from the Holy Spirit

Hey, sweet girl! I have an amazing story for you, one I hope you will remember so that you can tell others. One day, a long, long time ago, 120 Christians were gathered in an upstairs room together, praying. They were waiting on Me to do something amazing. I had promised them I would surprise them, and boy, did I show up in a big way!

That very day I sent My Holy Spirit into the room, and some amazing things began to happen. Tongues of fire appeared over their heads, and people began to speak in different languages, all at once. (Can you even imagine what would happen if you suddenly started speaking in French or Spanish or German?)

Oh, I wish you could've seen it! It was the coolest thing ever! They also (very suddenly) became super-duper bold. Being filled with the Spirit will do that for you! All of the people there were filled to the top with courage that only My Spirit can give. They started sharing the Gospel (the story of what I did on the cross) with others.

That's what happens when you become My

kid. I give you My Holy Spirit, and you're filled with power and might. Gone are the days of fear and worry. *Zap!* All that stuff goes away when My Spirit shows up. When that happens, you are able to do amazing things—great and mighty things—for Me.

Where does your courage come from? May it always come from Me. I will fill you up to the tippy-top!

As they were gathered together with Him,
He told them, "Do not leave Jerusalem.
Wait for what the Father has promised.
You heard Me speak of this. For John the
Baptist baptized with water but in a few days
you will be baptized with the Holy Spirit."
Those who were with Him asked, "Lord, is this
the time for You to give the nation back to the
Jews?" He said, "It is not for you to know
the special days or the special times which
the Father has put in His own power. But you
will receive power when the Holy Spirit comes
into your life. You will tell about Me in the city
of Jerusalem and over all the countries of
Judea and Samaria and to the ends of the earth."
ACTS 1:4–8

Stuff

Some people chase after money like a dog chases after its own tail. They want it. . .at any cost. In fact, some folks would do just about anything to get rich so that they can buy, buy, buy! They can't wait to get the latest, greatest phones, computers, clothes, or cars.

I want you to know that you don't have to be like that. Material possessions (cars, houses, fancy clothes, jewelry, electronics) are nice, but they shouldn't be the things you crave. Instead, you need to be consumed with Me!

Now, let's get real for a minute, because I can see you have some questions about what I'm saying. It's true; the people you hang out with . . .they like their stuff. They like it. . .a lot. And you like your stuff too. I'm not asking you to get rid of it. I'm not saying, "Stop going to the mall!" or "Stop spending your birthday money on toys and clothes." I'm just saying, "Hey, could you put that video game down long enough to spend a little time with Me? I'll make it worth your while, I promise!"

It takes courage to be your own person and not to chase after material possessions. After all, it's very satisfying to get that new outfit or that brand-new phone. But you'll be content so much longer if you focus on Me, not your stuff.

A God-like life gives us much when we are happy for what we have. We came into this world with nothing. For sure, when we die, we will take nothing with us. If we have food and clothing, let us be happy. But men who want lots of money are tempted. They are trapped into doing all kinds of foolish things and things which hurt them. These things drag them into sin and will destroy them. The love of money is the beginning of all kinds of sin. Some people have turned from the faith because of their love for money. They have made much pain for themselves because of this. But you, man of God, turn away from all these sinful things. Work at being right with God. Live a God-like life. Have faith and love. Be willing to wait. Have a kind heart. Fight the good fight of faith. Take hold of the life that lasts forever. You were chosen to receive it. You have spoken well about this life in front of many people.
1 Timothy 6:6–12

Fighting Giants

Hey, kiddo! If you've read My book (the Bible), you might already know the story of David and Goliath. I'll refresh your memory, in case you've forgotten.

I'll start by telling you about Goliath. He was a giant of a man! Goliath was more than nine feet tall, and everyone was terrified of him! (Sometimes I build 'em big!) If you met him face-to-face, your knees would be knocking, for sure!

Goliath wasn't a very nice guy. He didn't like My people, the Israelites. In fact, he planned to kill them. He stood across the battle lines and yelled mean things at them, like, "I'm going to take you out!"

A young shepherd boy named David showed up at the battle lines. He took one look at that horrible loudmouth of a giant and got mad! (Do you ever get mad when people are hollering mean things at you?) Even though he was just a boy, David wasn't scared of this beast of a man! He knew I was on his side. He took five smooth stones, put one of them in his slingshot, and killed that giant dead.

You might wonder what this story has to do with you. Just like David, you'll face some "giants" in your life. Here are a few you might be fretting over: worry, anger, jealousy, depression, or fear. Here are a few others: mean kids, bullies, and pop quizzes!

You can do what David did. Tell those giants that they have to go! I'm totally on your side!

And when the Philistine looked and saw David, he disdained him, for he was but a youth, ruddy and handsome in appearance. And the Philistine said to David, "Am I a dog, that you come to me with sticks?" And the Philistine cursed David by his gods. The Philistine said to David, "Come to me, and I will give your flesh to the birds of the air and to the beasts of the field." Then David said to the Philistine, "You come to me with a sword and with a spear and with a javelin, but I come to you in the name of the Lord of hosts, the God of the armies of Israel, whom you have defied. This day the Lord will deliver you into my hand, and I will strike you down and cut off your head. And I will give the dead bodies of the host of the Philistines this day to the birds of the air and to the wild beasts of the earth, that all the earth may know that there is a God in Israel, and that all this assembly may know that the Lord saves not with sword and spear. For the battle is the Lord's, and he will give you into our hand."

1 Samuel 17:42–47 esv

Even Now

I want you to be brave, even in the hard times. Like. . .even in the really, *really* hard times. Like that time your grandfather got really bad news from the doctor. Or that time your parents got into that big argument and you worried they would break up. Or that time when your best friend's mom lost her job and they didn't have money to pay the rent.

I don't want you to worry when these things happen. Don't be afraid. Don't give up your hope. I really mean that. . .I want you to be brave, no matter how hard things get. This won't be easy, but you're My daughter, and I'll give you the courage you need, even in the hardest moments. I will strengthen you. (I'm better than any energy drink!) I'll help you. (I'm better than even the toughest police officer.) I will hold you up with My right hand. That means I'll never be far away when you're going through tough stuff.

Trust Me. Stick with Me. Don't hyperfocus on the problems, even when they feel like they're too much to handle. Even then, keep your eyes on Me, and I'll give you the courage you need to make it through.

I promise. And I never ever go back on My promises.

But you, Israel, my servant, Jacob, whom I have chosen, the offspring of Abraham, my friend; you whom I took from the ends of the earth, and called from its farthest corners, saying to you, "You are my servant, I have chosen you and not cast you off"; fear not, for I am with you; be not dismayed, for I am your God; I will strengthen you, I will help you, I will uphold you with my righteous right hand. Behold, all who are incensed against you shall be put to shame and confounded; those who strive against you shall be as nothing and shall perish. You shall seek those who contend with you, but you shall not find them; those who war against you shall be as nothing at all. For I, the LORD your God, hold your right hand; it is I who say to you, "Fear not, I am the one who helps you."

ISAIAH 41:8–13 ESV

The Day I Died

I've already shared a little bit about the day I died on the cross and took away all of your sins, but I think you can handle the whole story now. It was a tough day for Me. . .the toughest ever. But it was all done out of love for you.

It started when My accusers mocked Me and beat Me. (Imagine the worst fight you've ever seen on the playground. It was much worse than that.) Afterward, these bullies made Me carry My cross all the way up the hill. I could barely make it, I was so exhausted. In fact, I dropped the cross and someone had to pick it up for Me.

When I reached the top of the hill, they nailed Me to a cross. I'll leave out the details, but let's just say it was very, very painful—ten thousand times worse than any pain you've ever felt. I was still thinking of you, though, even when they were hurting Me. I loved you so much that I wanted to do this for you.

Later that day—after lots of painful hours—I finally died. (I know, I know! You're wondering how I could be telling you this story if I'm dead!)

Well, the cool thing is I came back to life three days later!

My death on the cross was so hard, and I had to be really brave. You will have to do a lot of brave things in your life too, but you will never have to do anything as brave as what I did on that difficult day.

From noon until three o'clock it was dark over all the land. At three o'clock Jesus cried with a loud voice, "My God, My God, why have You left Me alone?" When some of those who stood by heard that, they said, "Listen! He is calling for Elijah." One of them ran and took a sponge and filled it with sour wine. He put it on a stick and gave it to Him to drink. He said, "Let Him alone. Let us see if Elijah will come and take Him down." Then Jesus gave a loud cry. He gave up His spirit and died. The curtain in the house of God was torn in two from top to bottom. The captain of the soldiers was looking at Jesus when He cried out. He saw Him die and said, "For sure, this Man was the Son of God."
MARK 15:33–39

It's Just a Feeling

Today I want to talk to you about something important. It's called loneliness. Loneliness is a feeling you get sometimes—when your friends don't include you, when your parents aren't around, or when you wonder if anyone likes you.

Here's what I want you to remember. Loneliness is just a feeling. Whenever you're feeling that way (all alone), just remember—I've made a promise to you that I will never leave you or forsake you. Never means never. When you're sitting alone in your room working on homework? I'm right there with you. When you're in bed at night, crying tears that no one sees. . .I see, and I care. I've sent My Spirit to live inside of you, to bring comfort and companionship.

Feelings will come and go. There's no way around that. But as soon as you start feeling lonely, just call on Me. Say something like, "Jesus, thank You for sticking close to me." And even though you can't see Me with your eyes, you'll feel Me with your heart. I promise. I'll give you the courage you need to get through the pain.

And I'm also giving you My Spirit, to make you very, very strong for moments like these.

So, keep the faith. Don't give up if you're feeling alone. You've got Me, kiddo, and I'm the best friend ever!

"If you love me, you will keep my commandments. And I will ask the Father, and he will give you another Helper, to be with you forever, even the Spirit of truth, whom the world cannot receive, because it neither sees him nor knows him. You know him, for he dwells with you and will be in you. I will not leave you as orphans; I will come to you. Yet a little while and the world will see me no more, but you will see Me. Because I live, you also will live. In that day you will know that I am in my Father, and you in me, and I in you."
JOHN 14:15–20 ESV

Big Things

Hey, you. Yes, you!

I want you to do big things for Me. *Really* big things.

What kind of things, you ask? I want you to figure out what talents you have and then develop them. After you develop them, I want you to use them for Me.

Still confused about what I mean?

Maybe you like to sing. Awesome! I love it when My kids make a joyful noise. Learn all you can about singing, and then one day you might stand up on the stage and lead worship at your church! Or maybe you are really good at science. Perfect! Learn all you can, and one day you can work in a laboratory and tell others about the miracles I've performed. Perhaps you love to write. You create amazing stories. Keep it up! Maybe one day you'll write books, telling others about how much I love them.

Think about My disciples. They were excellent fishermen. But once they started hanging out with Me, I taught them how to use that gift (fishing) to fish for souls (to tell others about Me).

No matter what you enjoy, no matter where you end up, remember: I've placed those talents and abilities inside of you. Whether it's dancing, acting, painting, writing, or making excellent grades in school, all of your super-spectacular talents come from Me. And you can use them to reach others, so that they can know Me too!

*To Timothy, my beloved child: Grace, mercy,
and peace from God the Father and Christ
Jesus our Lord. I thank God whom I serve,
as did my ancestors, with a clear conscience,
as I remember you constantly in my prayers
night and day. As I remember your tears, I long
to see you, that I may be filled with joy. I am
reminded of your sincere faith, a faith that
dwelt first in your grandmother Lois and your
mother Eunice and now, I am sure, dwells in
you as well. For this reason I remind you to
fan into flame the gift of God, which is in
you through the laying on of my hands,
for God gave us a spirit not of fear but
of power and love and self-control.*

2 TIMOTHY 1:2–7 ESV

Confess What You've Done

You messed up. You didn't mean to, but you did. I know, because I saw the whole thing! You told a little white lie, and before long it grew and grew and grew. Your tiny lie blew up like a busted water balloon, creating a horrible mess. You hoped no one would ever find out the truth, but now you've been caught. Your mom knows you've been lying, and you feel sick inside. You wish you could take it all back, but it's too late.

Oh boy. This is a big one! If you look in My Word, (the Bible), you'll see that it doesn't go well for the person who hides her sins. It's better if you confess. Get it off your chest. Tell someone. And remember, you can always come to Me to confess. (I already know everything you've done anyway.)

When you confess and ask for My forgiveness, guess what? I forgive you, lickety-split! Right in that very moment your sin is washed away. Forgotten. I've tossed it as far as the east is from the west.

It's still a good idea to confess to your mom

or dad though. I know, I know. . .it's not going to be easy. But I promise, you'll feel so much better once you've got that off your chest.

Go on now. You know what you need to do.

Whoever misleads the upright into an evil way will fall into his own pit, but the blameless will have a goodly inheritance. A rich man is wise in his own eyes, but a poor man who has understanding will find him out. When the righteous triumph, there is great glory, but when the wicked rise, people hide themselves. Whoever conceals his transgressions will not prosper, but he who confesses and forsakes them will obtain mercy. Blessed is the one who fears the Lord always, but whoever hardens his heart will fall into calamity.
PROVERBS 28:10–14 ESV

I'm Your Bestie

Hey, sweet girl. I know you get a little jealous of the kids who hang out with their friends all the time. You wonder if you'll ever know what that feels like. You watch as they go to the mall together or out to eat. You look on as they plan birthday parties you won't get to attend or trips to the beach you won't get to go on. And it makes you sad. *Very* sad. Why doesn't someone invite you to do those things?

Today's verse is all the proof you will ever need that someone wants to be your friend. That someone is Me! *I* am for you, so who can be against you? It doesn't matter how many people don't seem to like you—I adore you and call you My own. I will always be on your side, for you are My precious daughter.

You'll never find a better friend than Me, no matter how hard you search! And yes, I see how hard you've been searching for friends. You've tried to make friends with lots of people, but it doesn't always work out.

That's okay, girl! Not everyone is going to

want to be your friend. In fact, some people probably won't be friendly to you at all. . .and that's all right. Not everyone is meant to be a bestie. That's My job, after all!

P.S. There are a lot of kids who need a friend. Today, why not invite one of them over to hang out?

♡ ♥ ♥ ♡ ♥ ♥

We know that God makes all things work together for the good of those who love Him and are chosen to be a part of His plan. God knew from the beginning who would put their trust in Him. So He chose them and made them to be like His Son. Christ was first and all those who belong to God are His brothers. He called to Himself also those He chose. Those He called, He made right with Himself. Then He shared His shining-greatness with those He made right with Himself. What can we say about all these things? Since God is for us, who can be against us? God did not keep His own Son for Himself but gave Him for us all. Then with His Son, will He not give us all things?

ROMANS 8:28–32

Face the Scary Thing

Everything in your life is going great. Then. . . *bam!* From out of nowhere, a big problem comes along. A scary problem. It's worse than any horror movie you might have seen and ten times more frightening! Maybe someone you know is really, really sick, or your parents tell you they can't afford the mortgage on the house anymore so you'll have to move. Or worse, they think you might end up moving in with a family member until Dad finds a new job.

These big surprises can be overwhelming, and it's tempting to turn and run. That's how a lot of people handle tough situations, but I have a better solution: face the problem. That's right. Look it squarely in the eye and say, "You're not gonna take me down!"

I never meant for you to hide away from troubles. They will come and (with My strength) you'll get through them. It's not going to be easy. I never said it would be. But, together, we can do it.

Kiddo, remember: I haven't given you a spirit of fear. Instead, I'll fill you up with courage when you need it! I'll give you a spirit of power, love, and a sound mind too. Through My power (and not your own), you can bravely face any scary thing that comes your way!

Open those eyes. Don't hide. Let's face it together.

For this reason, I ask you to keep using the gift God gave you. It came to you when I laid my hands on you and prayed that God would use you. For God did not give us a spirit of fear. He gave us a spirit of power and of love and of a good mind. Do not be ashamed to tell others about what our Lord said, or of me here in prison. I am here because of Jesus Christ. Be ready to suffer for preaching the Good News and God will give you the strength you need. He is the One Who saved us from the punishment of sin. He is the One Who chose us to do His work. It is not because of anything we have done. But it was His plan from the beginning that He would give us His loving-favor through Christ Jesus.

2 TIMOTHY 1:6–9

My Power Is Working!

I know how much you love movies, girl! You're addicted! And it's fun to watch movies about superheroes, for sure. It's amazing to see them climb up the sides of buildings or fly through the air. You watch with your heart *thump-thump*ing as they leap across skyscrapers and take out the bad guys. Wow, they're really something, aren't they?

I know you inside and out, sweet girl, and I know that you secretly wish you had those amazing, superhuman powers too! You wish you could accomplish great feats. Well, here's some good news: you can!

If you really want to see something supernatural, hang out with Me. Girl, I can heal the sick, make the blind see, fix broken relationships, and even raise people from the dead! (Are you amazed yet?) There's no superhero in any movie who even comes close to Me. They can fly through the air, but I created the air. . .and I'm everywhere, all at once.

I can do more than you could ask or think. Just read today's Bible verse for proof. And guess what? I want to work *through* you! That means you will become a superhero when My Spirit lives and works inside of you. You probably can't imagine that's even possible, but it is. When I breathe My strength and courage into you, you're even more amazing than Wonder Woman!

We've got exciting things to do together, kiddo. Let's get busy and watch miracles take place.

For this reason, I bow my knees and pray to the Father. It is from Him that every family in heaven and on earth has its name. I pray that because of the riches of His shining-greatness, He will make you strong with power in your hearts through the Holy Spirit. I pray that Christ may live in your hearts by faith. I pray that you will be filled with love. I pray that you will be able to understand how wide and how long and how high and how deep His love is. I pray that you will know the love of Christ. His love goes beyond anything we can understand. I pray that you will be filled with God Himself. God is able to do much more than we ask or think through His power working in us. May we see His shining-greatness in the church. May all people in all time honor Christ Jesus. Let it be so.

EPHESIANS 3:14–21

Wake up, Sleepyhead!

Yawn! Stretch! Roll over in the bed. Cover your head with the blanket to keep the morning sunlight away. Do you really have to get up? Would anyone notice if you just kept snoozing?

I know, I know! It's tempting just to chill, to rest, to take the day off. But sometimes (please don't take this personally) I notice that you're a little, well, lazy.

Remember that time Mom asked you to clean up the toys in your room? You didn't really feel like doing it so you moved v-e-r-y s-l-o-w-l-y . . . . Like a snail. I know, because I was watching. You didn't exactly give it your best effort. In fact, (just keeping it real!) you were hardly giving it any effort at all!

Half an hour later the room still looked like a hot mess. And when Mom came in to ask, "What in the world were you doing in here?" You just shrugged because, after all, you weren't doing much.

Kiddo, let's talk about this. I want you to work with your whole heart, every bit of it. I want you to perform every task as if you were doing it for Me. It will take courage and strength, but together we'll accomplish so much! So, push those covers back. Get out of that bed. We've got big stuff to do!

Children, obey your parents in everything. The Lord is pleased when you do. Fathers, do not be so hard on your children that they will give up trying to do what is right. You who are servants who are owned by someone, obey your owners. Work hard for them all the time, not just when they are watching you. Work for them as you would for the Lord because you honor God. Whatever work you do, do it with all your heart. Do it for the Lord and not for men. Remember that you will get your reward from the Lord. He will give you what you should receive. You are working for the Lord Christ. If anyone does wrong, he will suffer for it. God does not respect one person more than another.

Colossians 3:20–25

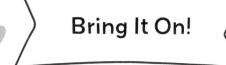

Bring It On!

I see how it is, kiddo. Sometimes you feel like giving up before you ever get started. Think about a time when your teacher or coach asked you to work on a difficult assignment. It seemed impossible, right? It was so tempting to give up. I seem to recall, you spent a lot more time whining and complaining than jumping in.

That's a normal response, by the way. Most kids freak out when they think the task is too big. Things can look pretty scary, after all. They just assume there's no way they can do it.

Here's a fun secret: facing the challenge and working through it will give you strength and courage you never knew you had! And here's another thing—the more times you face these obstacles, the braver you get. Before long, you can look those problems in the eye and say, "Bring it on! I ain't scared of you!"

The next time you feel overwhelmed by the challenge in front of you, pray for courage and help in figuring things out. I'll be right there to help you, I promise. Just glance My way and say,

"Jesus, would You mind giving me a little courage to get this done?" I'll be happy to be of service.

No more complaining, sweet girl. Time to get busy! Bring it on!

I will honor the Lord at all times. His praise will always be in my mouth. My soul will be proud to tell about the Lord. Let those who suffer hear it and be filled with joy. Give great honor to the Lord with me. Let us praise His name together. I looked for the Lord, and He answered me. And He took away all my fears. They looked to Him and their faces shined with joy. Their faces will never be ashamed. This poor man cried, and the Lord heard him. And He saved him out of all his troubles. The angel of the Lord stays close around those who fear Him, and He takes them out of trouble.

PSALM 34:1–7

Courage Like Paul and Silas

All of My apostles (followers) were very brave, but today I want to tell you a special story about two of them—Paul and Silas. They were going from town to town, telling people about Me.

The people in one town didn't like what they were sharing, and so these two godly men were beaten and thrown into prison. (Can you imagine being jailed for your faith?) The jailer was given a command to keep a close eye on them. He put them in an inner cell, far away from any potential escape. Not that they planned to go anywhere. They were okay just hanging out in prison until I fixed the problem.

The guard wasn't counting on an earthquake! At midnight, as Paul and Silas were worshipping Me in song and prayer, an earthquake shook the place so violently that the chains busted! My guys were free to run, but chose to stay behind to talk to the guard and to share the story of how I could save him from his sins.

Here's the point: I want people to know who I am. And guess who's going to tell them? You!

You're just like Paul and Silas. You're My apostle. And I need you to be brave enough to speak up, even if people around you don't like what you're sharing. I'll be with you, no matter what!

Many people had gathered around Paul and Silas. They were calling out things against them. The leaders had the clothes of Paul and Silas taken off and had them beaten with sticks. After they had hit them many times, they put Paul and Silas in prison. The soldiers told the man who watched the prison to be sure to keep them from getting away. Because of this, they were put in the inside room of the prison and their feet were put in pieces of wood that held them. About midnight Paul and Silas were praying and singing songs of thanks to God. The other men in prison were listening to them. All at once the earth started to shake. The stones under the prison shook and the doors opened. The chains fell off from everyone.

Acts 16:22–26

Courage to Believe in Heaven

Some people believe that when you die, you no longer exist. They believe that once you're gone . . .you're gone. That's not true though. There's a place called heaven, and it's beyond anything you could imagine! Think of the most amazing beach you've ever visited. It's prettier than that. Think of the most gorgeous mountains you've ever seen. It's even lovelier than they are!

I prepared heaven for you and for all of the people who say yes to Me. To say "yes" means you accept Me as Lord and Savior of your life. You make Me the boss of everything. You pray a prayer like this: "Jesus, come and save me. Be my Lord and Savior. Forgive me of my sins. Take me to heaven with You one day! Amen!" In that very moment, you'll become Mine, and you can be sure you'll see heaven one day.

It takes courage to believe in a place you haven't seen, but I promise you, you'll see it when the right time comes. And you're going to love it! In heaven there are streets of gold, beautiful mansions, and even gates made of pearl. There's a crystal sea, and all around it, people are singing "Holy, holy, holy!" It's going to be an experience like you've never had, not even at the coolest amusement park.

Thank you for getting your heart ready for heaven, sweet girl. Now, go and share the news with others, so that they can come to heaven one day too.

"Do not let your heart be troubled. You have put your trust in God, put your trust in Me also. There are many rooms in My Father's house. If it were not so, I would have told you. I am going away to make a place for you. After I go and make a place for you, I will come back and take you with Me. Then you may be where I am. You know where I am going and you know how to get there." Thomas said to Jesus, "Lord, we do not know where You are going. How can we know the way to get there?" Jesus said, "I am the Way and the Truth and the Life. No one can go to the Father except by Me. If you had known Me, you would know My Father also. From now on you know Him and have seen Him."

JOHN 14:1–7

My Battle Record

Satan is the enemy of your soul. He's fighting hard to take you down. Sometimes it can seem like every day is one battle after another.

So, here's a question for you: How many battles do you *win*, compared to those you *lose*? (Some would call this your battle record.) When you look back over your life, would you say you're more a winner. . .or loser? No doubt you've seen the good and the bad!

Did you realize that I have the best track record of all? Every battle I enter into, I win. Nobody else on the planet can say that. No one has My track record or My awesome power. There's a victory every single time, as long as I'm the One doing the fighting. Wow! Remarkable, right?

Knowing that should bring you great peace. You can rest easy, knowing that it's not your track record that matters. Even if you feel like a total loser, it's not your record you need to be concerned about. You can put your trust in My work, not your own. Whew! That has to feel good!

Just one little problem, girl. I've noticed you

don't always let Me fight your battles for you. Sometimes you like to fight them on your own. That's okay. You're learning to let go and place things in My hands. When you do that, you'll have one victory after another.

"When you go to battle against those who hate you and see more horses and war-wagons and soldiers than you have, do not be afraid of them. For the Lord your God, Who brought you from the land of Egypt, is with you. When you are coming near the battle, the religious leader will come near and speak to the people. He will say to them, 'Hear, O Israel. Today you are going into battle against those who hate you. Do not let your hearts become weak. Do not be afraid and shake in fear before them. For the Lord your God is the One Who goes with you. He will fight for you against those who hate you. And He will save you.'"

DEUTERONOMY 20:1–4

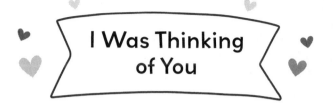

I Was Thinking of You

When I hung the moon and the stars in the sky, I was thinking of you. I knew that their twinkle and shine would make your heart happy. And when I took the time to create snow-capped mountains and rushing rivers, I was also thinking of you. I thought, "She's gonna love this!" And don't even get Me started on rainbows! I just knew you were going to be filled with hope if you could catch a glimpse of those brilliant colors after a thunderstorm.

I took the time to create caterpillars and dragonflies, bunny rabbits and porcupines. And even though I was super busy with all of that, I decided the world needed a girl like you. So I made you. . .you. Your hair. Your eyes. Your special smile. Your sweet personality. And I put you in the perfect-for-you family, so that you could grow into an awesome, godly woman.

I'm pretty busy, taking care of creation, but sweet girl. . .I never stop thinking about you. I'm so glad I created you. I love and adore you so much.

Doesn't it make you feel good to know I was thinking of you when I created heaven and earth? And now for a little secret: as much as I love the animals, the rivers, and all of nature. . .I love you even more.

O Lord, our Lord, how great is Your name in all the earth. You have set Your shining-greatness above the heavens. Out of the mouth of children and babies, You have built up strength because of those who hate You, and to quiet those who fight against You. When I look up and think about Your heavens, the work of Your fingers, the moon and the stars, which You have set in their place, what is man, that You think of him, the son of man that You care for him? You made him a little less than the angels and gave him a crown of greatness and honor. You made him to rule over the works of Your hands. You put all things under his feet: All sheep and cattle, all the wild animals, the birds of the air, and the fish of the sea, and all that pass through the sea. O Lord, our Lord, how great is Your name in all the earth!
PSALM 8:1–9

When You're Weak, I Am Strong!

Girl, I know you have bad days. I've witnessed them! Some mornings you crawl out of bed feeling like a real weakling. You're like Popeye the Sailor Man before he's had his spinach! You're tired. You're cranky. You want to give up before you start. But you decide to keep going, sure the day will get better. Only, it doesn't. You have a rough day in school. By the time you get home, you're ready to plop onto the sofa and give up. Every part of your day has been a giant flop.

So, what do I expect My kids to do on those weak days? Do I want you to give up, to crawl under the covers? Nope! That's not the solution, though I'm sure it does sound tempting. Those are the days when I want to show up in a big way and to prove that I've got your back. I'm here to remind you that I'm the one with the super-charged power from on high. When you're weak, I'm loaded with supernatural strength. And when you say, "I can't!" I'll say, "I can!" You can trust Me with this. I won't let you down.

Don't give up. I'm the strongest of the strong,

and I want to work through you. Put your faith in Me, even when you're feeling like a weakling.

*The things God showed me were so great.
But to keep me from being too full of pride
because of seeing these things, I have been
given trouble in my body. It was sent from
Satan to hurt me. It keeps me from being
proud. I asked the Lord three times to take it
away from me. He answered me, "I am all you
need. I give you My loving-favor. My power
works best in weak people." I am happy to be
weak and have troubles so I can have Christ's
power in me. I receive joy when I am weak.
I receive joy when people talk against me and
make it hard for me and try to hurt me and
make trouble for me. I receive joy when all
these things come to me because of Christ.
For when I am weak, then I am strong.*
2 CORINTHIANS 12:7–10

Words Give Courage

Sometimes people say nice things about you when you're young and you remember them as you grow up. Maybe someone once said, "You're so smart!" or perhaps someone said, "I really love the way you sing. I bet you'll lead worship one day or sing on the radio!"

When people say nice things about you, you remember them. Their words give you confidence. They make you feel brave, as if you're really capable of doing what they said.

Today's Bible verse is about a young man named Timothy. Many wonderful things were spoken over him when he was a boy, and these words gave him courage as he grew older. He became a missionary and traveled from place to place telling others about Jesus. He went on to do amazing things for the Lord, even though he was younger than the other disciples. (No one looked down on him because he was young, by the way. They thought he was pretty remarkable!)

What kind words have been spoken over you? Stop to think. . .really think. What did your grandmother say? What did your teacher say? What about your mom or dad, or maybe your coach?

Never forget that God has fabulous things for you to do if you just have the courage to believe. Keep those sweet words in mind as you grow up, and watch as the Lord brings them to pass.

What I say is true and all the world should receive it. Christ Jesus came into the world to save sinners from their sin and I am the worst sinner. And yet God had loving-kindness for me. Jesus Christ used me to show how long He will wait for even the worst sinners. In that way, others will know they can have life that lasts forever also. We give honor and thanks to the King Who lives forever. He is the One Who never dies and Who is never seen. He is the One Who knows all things. He is the only God. Let it be so. Timothy, my son, here is my word to you. Fight well for the Lord! God's preachers told us you would. Keep a strong hold on your faith in Christ. May your heart always say you are right. Some people have not listened to what their hearts say. They have done what they knew was wrong. Because of this, their faith in Christ was wrecked.

1 TIMOTHY 1:15–19

New Kid in the Room

It's not easy being the new kid in town. Walking into a school classroom where nobody knows you is tough! Who should you sit by? Will they be nice to you?

It can be even harder if you're new to the neighborhood and want to play with the kids who already know each other. You might get scared or even want to chicken out. But remember, I'm going before you. I'll be like your bodyguard, so you don't have to be afraid of meeting the new people. I can help you get over the fear, I promise.

Let's try this: instead of panicking (I know you want to!), just put a smile on your face, turn to someone new, and say, "Hi! I'm so-and-so." (Insert your real name, of course. Don't say "so-and-so.") Say, "I'm new." You might just be surprised to see that you're greeted with warmth and kindness if you act brave. And as you get to know those new people, you might also learn that you have a lot in common with them, maybe even more than you imagined!

You'll never know if you don't try. So, take a

deep breath. Lift those shoulders! Put your trust in Me, and trust Me when I say, "These people are going to *love* you!"

I praise the Word of God. I have put my trust in God. I will not be afraid. What can only a man do to me? All day long they change my words to say what I did not say. They are always thinking of ways to hurt me. They go after me as in a fight. They hide themselves. They watch my steps, as they have waited to take my life. Because they are bad, do not let them get away. Bring down the people in Your anger, O God. You have seen how many places I have gone. Put my tears in Your bottle. Are they not in Your book? Then those who hate me will turn back when I call. I know that God is for me. I praise the Word of God. I praise the Word of the Lord. In God I have put my trust. I will not be afraid. What can man do to me? I am under an agreement with You, O God. I will give You gifts of thanks. For You have set my soul free from death. You have kept my feet from fall-ing, so I may walk with God in the light of life.

Psalm 56:4–13

Take a Stand for What's Right

You think I don't see everything that's going on, but I do. I see when you're trying super-duper hard and things still don't go your way. I see the sadness in your eyes when the situation takes a belly-flop.

Like that time you tried to share your faith with a friend in school and she made fun of you. Or that time you tried to start an after-school Bible study at school but no one showed up. Or that time your friend tried to get you to lie for her and you wouldn't. . .so she stopped hanging out with you.

It's frustrating, right? And it hurts even more when wicked people seem to get their way. *Ugh.* Life is like that at times. People take a stand for what's right but end up getting hurt. It stinks!

So what do you do when things don't turn out right for you? First of all, don't get discouraged. Don't get mad. In this life, things won't always work out the way you hope. Don't forget to turn to Me. I'll be right there to give you courage, strength, and wisdom, even if you're feeling hopeless.

Here's something else to keep in mind: one

day you will live in heaven with Me. There, everything will be made right. You won't have to worry about standing up for what's right, because up here, *everything* is right.

"Those who know there is nothing good in themselves are happy, because the holy nation of heaven is theirs. Those who have sorrow are happy, because they will be comforted. Those who have no pride in their hearts are happy, because the earth will be given to them. Those who are hungry and thirsty to be right with God are happy, because they will be filled. Those who show loving-kindness are happy, because they will have loving-kindness shown to them. Those who have a pure heart are happy, because they will see God. Those who make peace are happy, because they will be called the sons of God. Those who have it very hard for doing right are happy, because the holy nation of heaven is theirs. You are happy when people act and talk in a bad way to you and make it very hard for you and tell bad things and lies about you because you trust in Me. Be glad and full of joy because your reward will be much in heaven. They made it very hard for the early preachers who lived a long time before you.

Matthew 5:3–12

Courage to Love Others as You Love Yourself

If you read My Word, you'll see that I've given you a couple of big commands: to love Me most of all and to love others as you love yourself. If you've asked Me into your heart (you have, haven't you?), then loving Me most of all is easy. But loving others as you love yourself? That's a little trickier. It's not always fun to put the needs of someone else above your own, especially if it means you have to sacrifice something.

Here's an example: your school is doing a play. You're trying out for a big part, and you really think you might get it. Your friend is talented too, and she's never had a big part before. You both audition for the same part, and you have a hard time feeling happy for her when she gets it. (Don't deny it, girl! I can see inside your heart, so I know what you were really thinking when the music teacher made the announcement!)

I want you to celebrate your friend's accomplishments and wish her the very best, even if it means you don't get what you want. It's hard, but in the end you'll be so happy you loved her as much as you love yourself. And don't forget, I've got lots of other things in store for you. . . opportunities to do great things. Your turn will come. For now, give that friend a big round of applause!

The proud religious law-keepers got together when they heard that the religious group of people who believe no one will be raised from the dead were not able to talk anymore to Jesus. A proud religious law-keeper who knew the Law tried to trap Jesus. He said, "Teacher, which one is the greatest of the Laws?" Jesus said to him, "'You must love the Lord your God with all your heart and with all your soul and with all your mind.' This is the first and greatest of the Laws. The second is like it, 'You must love your neighbor as you love yourself.' All the Laws and the writings of the early preachers depend on these two most important Laws."
MATTHEW 22:34–40

Loving the Haters

It's easy to love people who are kind to you, but I am going to ask you to do something a lot harder—I want you to love those who hate you. Ouch! (I know, right? It seems impossible, especially with some people!) But I'm right here to help you with this, so you won't be on your own.

I have a few tips for how you can love those who seem unlovable. You can start by not doing paybacks. If someone hurts you, don't hurt them back. (Told you it wasn't going to be easy!) If they're mean, respond in love. You might think I don't know how hard this is, but I do! Remember, many people were cruel to Me and even wanted to see Me dead! I loved them anyway. . .so much that I went to the cross for them.

Next, don't talk ugly about the mean kids behind their backs. This is going to be tough, but remember. . .I love those people very much. (Does it shock you to hear that I love the meanies? Maybe that seems a little unfair to you, that I would love everyone the same. But it's true! I gave My life for them too.)

Most of all, pray for them. They need your prayers more than you know. And you know what? I can't wait to hear you lift their names up in prayer, girl.

You can do this. Just go on loving as I've taught you to love.

"I say to you who hear Me, love those who work against you. Do good to those who hate you. Respect and give thanks for those who try to bring bad to you. Pray for those who make it very hard for you. Whoever hits you on one side of the face, turn so he can hit the other side also. Whoever takes your coat, give him your shirt also. Give to any person who asks you for something. If a person takes something from you, do not ask for it back. Do for other people what you would like to have them do for you. If you love those who love you, what pay can you expect from that? Sinners also love those who love them. If you do good to those who do good to you, what pay can you expect from that? Sinners also do good to those who do good to them."

Luke 6:27–33

Let's All Get Along

Working in the church nursery can be a lot of fun. Hanging out with little kids is the best! And you've had lots of experience helping care for them—at church, at home (your own brothers and sisters), at family outings (cousins), or even at your best friend's house (watching her little sister).

Yes, caring for little ones is fun. . .but it can also be a pain. Whenever you put a lot of kids together in one space, sometimes they begin to squabble and fight. Oh, not you, of course. You would never do that. (Kidding! I've seen you do it!) Some kids just don't get along well in a group.

Why do you think kids argue when they get together in groups? Because every single one wants his or her own way. When you get that many people all demanding their own way, things can get crazy in a hurry! (Trust Me, I've heard a lot of prayers from people saying, "Jesus, please make my kid sister nicer!")

What if people stopped demanding their own way? What if everyone said, "That's okay. We can do it your way instead of my way." Wow! People would start getting along for sure. And that's exactly what I hope you'll do. Instead of squabbling when you don't get your way, you can honor Me by letting someone else have a turn.

Ah, how good and pleasant it is when My kids get along!

See, how good and how pleasing it is for brothers to live together as one! It is like oil of great worth poured on the head, flowing down through the hair on the face, even the face of Aaron, and flowing down to his coat. It is like the morning water of Hermon coming down upon the hills of Zion. For there the Lord has given the gift of life that lasts forever. See, give honor and thanks to the Lord, all who work for the Lord, who stand during the night in the house of the Lord. Lift up your hands to the holy place and give thanks to the Lord. May the Lord bring good to you from Zion. He is the One Who made heaven and earth.

PSALM 133:1–134:3

Guardian Angels

Wouldn't you love to be an angel for a day? I spend a lot of time with them, and I can tell you, they're pretty amazing! I guess you'll just have to trust Me with this one, but here's one little hint: they're a *lot* more fantabulous than the costumes you see at Christmastime. They're big and strong and guard you while you play and even while you sleep.

I know what you're thinking: it would be amazing to see what they see and do what they do. After all, angels get to spend time in My presence and still see what's going on with humans as well. They really get around!

Look around you. Do you see any angels right now? Can you feel the flutter of their wings? No? Well, I see them! My Word says that I command My angels to guard you in all of your ways. That means you are surrounded by angels who were put there to protect you, even at this very moment. (Cool, right?) You might not be able to see them, but they are standing guard even now. Wow, what an amazing thought!

I care so much about you that I want to protect you. I've given My angels charge over you, so rest easy! They've got you covered, even when you're scared.

Because you have made the Lord your safe place, and the Most High the place where you live, nothing will hurt you. No trouble will come near your tent. For He will tell His angels to care for you and keep you in all your ways. They will hold you up in their hands. So your foot will not hit against a stone. You will walk upon the lion and the snake. You will crush under your feet the young lion and the snake. Because he has loved Me, I will bring him out of trouble. I will set him in a safe place on high, because he has known My name. He will call upon Me, and I will answer him. I will be with him in trouble. I will take him out of trouble and honor him. I will please him with a long life. And I will show him My saving power.

Psalm 91:9–16

Believe, Even When You Can't See

You can't see Me with your eyes, so how do you know I'm really there? When someone asks you, "How do you know God is real?" do you answer with confidence, or do you pause, worried they won't believe you, since you have no visible proof?

Believing without seeing is where faith comes in. You can see Me with your heart. You can see the wonderful things I've done for your family and friends.

Think about the wind. You can feel it blow, but can you see it? Nope. You can see the leaves tumbling down from the trees, so you have the proof. The same is true with Me. You can't see Me, but you can see the things I'm doing in your life and in the lives of your family members. In other words, you see the proof through My actions.

Believing in Me takes faith and courage. Take a look at today's verse. I love it when you take Me at My word. It makes Me so happy when you believe in Me even though you can't see Me with your eyes.

Kiddo, I'm doing great and mighty things in your life. You can't see them yet, but someday you will. When you are grown up you will look back on your life and say, "Wow! The Lord did some amazing things in me."

Now faith is being sure we will get what we hope for. It is being sure of what we cannot see. God was pleased with the men who had faith who lived long ago. Through faith we understand that the world was made by the Word of God. Things we see were made from what could not be seen. Because Abel had faith, he gave a better gift in worship to God than Cain. His gift pleased God. Abel was right with God. Abel died, but by faith he is still speaking to us. Because Enoch had faith, he was taken up from the earth without dying. He could not be found because God had taken him. The Holy Writings tell how he pleased God before he was taken up. A man cannot please God unless he has faith. Anyone who comes to God must believe that He is. That one must also know that God gives what is promised to the one who keeps on looking for Him.

HEBREWS 11:1–6

Courageous Laughter

Remember that time you got really, really sick? You had a bad cold and high fever. And then there was that time when you had a stomach bug. Mom took great care of you, but you just wanted to feel well again! Being sick is so icky! You have to stay in bed, and you feel just awful. You wonder if you'll ever feel good again.

When you're really sick, the doctor prescribes medicine for you to take. (Hint: I gave that doctor the wisdom to study hard so that he could take care of My kids!) The medicine he gives you helps you get better quicker. If you refuse to take it, you could be sick for a long time, or even get worse.

I have special medicine too. You won't find it at the drug store or in the medicine cabinet. Mom's not hiding it in the cupboard, so don't bother looking there. My medicine isn't something you swallow in your mouth. It's called laughter! (It's true—laughter is medicine!) When you're happy, you start to feel better inside and out. And I love it when My kids laugh, especially when things aren't going their way.

The next time you get the giggles, look up to heaven and say, "Thanks for my meds, Lord! I feel better already!"

I will give honor and thanks to the Lord, Who has told me what to do. Yes, even at night my mind teaches me. I have placed the Lord always in front of me. Because He is at my right hand, I will not be moved. And so my heart is glad. My soul is full of joy. My body also will rest without fear. For You will not give me over to the grave. And You will not allow Your Holy One to return to dust. You will show me the way of life. Being with You is to be full of joy. In Your right hand there is happiness forever.
PSALM 16:7–11

No Paybacks, Girl!

Oh, how you want to get even! That boy on the bus called you a terrible name, and you're tempted to get in his face and call him a name or two. But you don't. You remember this verse from 1 Peter about praying for those who hurt you. *Ugh.* You don't want to pray for him. You want to get even.

Getting even isn't how I roll, kiddo. But then again, you already knew that, right? I mean, we've been talking for a while now, and I've already told you to love others as you love yourself, which means you can't respond to anyone in anger. Instead, just take a deep breath and ask for My help when things like this happen.

I want you to release your anger and pain to Me and to trust that I will take care of things in My own way and My own time. It's not easy. In fact, living like this is very, very hard at times and takes a lot of self-control and courage. But I promise I will give you the ability to calm yourself down, even when you're really mad. And I'll give you the courage you need not to get even.

No paybacks, kiddo. No getting even. Just. . . love.

♡ ♥ ♥ ♡ ♥ ♥

Last of all, you must share the same thoughts and the same feelings. Love each other with a kind heart and with a mind that has no pride. When someone does something bad to you, do not do the same thing to him. When someone talks about you, do not talk about him. Instead, pray that good will come to him. You were called to do this so you might receive good things from God. For "If you want joy in your life and have happy days, keep your tongue from saying bad things and your lips from talking bad about others. Turn away from what is sinful. Do what is good. Look for peace and go after it. The Lord watches over those who are right with Him. He hears their prayers. But the Lord is against those who sin."

1 PETER 3:8–12

Serve Me Courageously

I've gotta be honest with you, sweet girl. It doesn't feel good to be disobeyed. Not everyone loves Me and wants to follow Me. Lots of people deliberately choose to disobey Me. Sure, there are times when you want to go along with the crowd and do the wrong thing too. But I know you. You're an amazing, godly girl—one who loves Me and loves others. So you resist the temptation. You've already learned that serving Me isn't always easy, but doing the right thing pleases My heart. (And you love to please Me, I know!)

Yes, it takes lots of courage to stand up and do the right thing. Sure, you'll have people in the crowd who think you're crazy for making godly decisions. . .but make them anyway. I'll help you, I promise.

Here's a question: If every single person in your world turned their back on Me, would you? Nope. I know you, girl! You'd still keep following Me, living courageously. And I'm incredibly happy when you do.

Take a stand for things that are right. Run

from things that are wrong. And most of all, don't get nervous if your opinion is different from everyone else's. That's going to happen sometimes. You just stick to what you know is true.

"So fear the Lord. Serve Him in faith and truth. Put away the gods your fathers served on the other side of the river and in Egypt. Serve the Lord. If you think it is wrong to serve the Lord, choose today whom you will serve. Choose the gods your fathers worshiped on the other side of the river, or choose the gods of the Amorites in whose land you are living. But as for me and my family, we will serve the Lord." The people answered, "May it never be that we turn away from the Lord and serve other gods. For the Lord our God is the One Who brought us and our fathers out of the land of Egypt, from the house where we were made to work. He did these powerful works in front of our eyes. He kept us safe everywhere we went, among all the nations we passed through. The Lord drove away from in front of us all the nations, even the Amorites who lived in the land. So we will serve the Lord. For He is our God."

Joshua 24:14–18

Never Stop Praying

I can tell you get really worried sometimes. You start to panic. You're not sure what to do. You just stand there, frozen in place.

I have good news for you, sweet girl. You never have to give in to worry or fear. Just come to Me. Right away. As soon as you start to get afraid, just come running straight to Me.

You can start by telling Me what's going on. (I already know, by the way, but it's nice to hear you share your heart.) When you've told Me everything you're worried about, I jump into action! I'm like a ninja warrior, only faster. *Whoosh!* With one breath I can *Zap! Pow! Bam!* your problem.

Maybe you say, "I don't really know how to talk to You, God. It's hard because I can't see You!"

That's okay! Talk to Me, anyway. Say it in your heart or say it out loud. Doesn't matter to Me. Nothing fancy-schmancy. You don't need to add a bunch of *Thees* and *Thous*. Just say it. Let Me know when something is up, and I'll be right there to calm your fears and give you peace.

P.S. Did you know that prayer is a two-way street? When you talk to Me, I talk back! You'll have to listen closely to hear the words I whisper to your heart, but if you're really tuned in, You'll hear Me. So never stop praying.

Be full of joy all the time. Never stop praying. In everything give thanks. This is what God wants you to do because of Christ Jesus. Do not try to stop the work of the Holy Spirit. Do not laugh at those who speak for God. Test everything and do not let good things get away from you. Keep away from everything that even looks like sin. May the God of peace set you apart for Himself. May every part of you be set apart for God. May your spirit and your soul and your body be kept complete. May you be without blame when our Lord Jesus Christ comes again.

1 Thessalonians 5:16–23

Beautiful Feet

What girl doesn't like a pedicure? It's so relaxing and fun to stick your feet in the warm, bubbly water for a soak. Ahh! And how wonderful to get that foot massage, complete with lotion. While your nails are being painted, you're not thinking about anything else, just how exciting it will be to show off your pretty toenails in some cute sandals or barefoot at the pool.

Here's some fun news: even if you never have a pedicure in your entire life, your feet will still be beautiful to Me. It's true! Take a close look at today's verse. When you travel here and there, sharing the good news of what I've done in your life, your feet look beautiful to Me.

When was the last time you shared the good news with someone? When was the last time you said, "Jesus can help you with that problem! He can save you, bring you happiness and peace! He can set you free."

Are you nervous about sharing that message? Worried about what they'll say? Remember, it's called "good" news for a reason. It's meant to be shared!

No worries! Just take those pedicured feet and point them in the direction of someone who needs to know how much I adore them. Share that good news, sweet girl. I'll take care of the rest.

How beautiful on the mountains are the feet of him who brings good news, who tells of peace and brings good news of happiness, who tells of saving power, and says to Zion, "Your God rules!" Listen! Your watchmen lift up their voices. They call out together for joy, for they will see with their own eyes the return of the Lord to Zion. Break out together into singing, you waste places of Jerusalem. For the Lord has comforted His people. He has saved Jerusalem. The Lord has shown His holy arm in the eyes of all the nations, that all the ends of the earth may see that our God saves.

Isaiah 52:7–10

Speak... and Act

You're a doer, girl! You're always on the move, doing this or that. Whew! You're one busy bee! I love that about you.

Since you love to "do," I thought I'd share something with you today. You know how you're always saying "I love you" to your mom, dad, siblings, or grandparents? They love it when you say that. I love it too. It brings Me great joy to hear those words come out of your mouth.

You know what gets Me even more excited? When you prove those words with your actions. Do you remember that time you said, "You're my BFF!" to your friend? But then you stopped hanging out with her or spending time with her. Did you follow through with your actions? Did she really sense your love? Nope!

If you care about the people in your life (and I know you do) then do things that will show them how much you care. Think about it this way: Would you believe your mom loved you if she said the words "I love you" but never fed you or gave you a place to live? Words need to be followed by actions. I want you to follow through, kiddo. Don't just say it. . .do it.

♡ 🖤 🖤 ♡ 🖤 🖤

We know what love is because Christ gave His life for us. We should give our lives for our brothers. What if a person has enough money to live on and sees his brother in need of food and clothing? If he does not help him, how can the love of God be in him? My children, let us not love with words or in talk only. Let us love by what we do and in truth. This is how we know we are Christians. It will give our heart comfort for sure when we stand before Him. Our heart may say that we have done wrong. But remember, God is greater than our heart. He knows everything. Dear friends, if our heart does not say that we are wrong, we will have no fear as we stand before Him. We will receive from Him whatever we ask if we obey Him and do what He wants. This is what He said we must do: Put your trust in the name of His Son, Jesus Christ, and love each other. Christ told us to do this.
1 John 3:16–23

Peace in the Storm

Here's a cool (true!) story. I was in a boat with My disciples, headed across the Sea of Galilee. I decided to go below deck and take a little nap. While I was snoozing, a huge storm blew up. I wasn't paying any attention because I needed My z's.

Up above Me, My disciples were completely panicked when the waves nearly flipped the boat over. They came busting into My room and woke Me up with the words, "Teacher, don't You care if we drown?"

Of course I cared! But I wanted to teach them a lesson about faith and how they could trust in Me, even when they couldn't see Me with their eyes. (Hey, I was enjoying My alone time!)

I went up to the top of the boat and took one look at that storm. It didn't seem like a huge deal to Me, but because it was worrying them, I said, "Peace, be still!" Right away the waves calmed down. The boat stopped rocking.

Now, My guys were completely in shock when this happened. But here's the truth: I wanted to prove to them that they could have courage, even in the middle of the storms of life. And I want you to know the very same thing, kiddo! No matter how hard the winds might blow, you're a girl of great courage!

It was evening of that same day. Jesus said to them, "Let us go over to the other side." After sending the people away, they took Jesus with them in a boat. It was the same boat He used when He taught them. Other little boats went along with them. A bad wind storm came up. The waves were coming over the side of the boat. It was filling up with water. Jesus was in the back part of the boat sleeping on a pillow. They woke Him up, crying out, "Teacher, do You not care that we are about to die?" He got up and spoke sharp words to the wind. He said to the sea, "Be quiet! Be still." At once the wind stopped blowing. There were no more waves. He said to His followers, "Why are you so full of fear? Do you not have faith?" They were very much afraid and said to each other, "Who is this? Even the wind and waves obey Him!"

MARK 4:35–41

Who Are You Trying to Please?

I've been thinking about something I want to share with you. Do you remember that time you had to sing a solo in front of your class? Remember how your knees shook and you felt terrified? After you were done you couldn't stop thinking about all of the mistakes you had made (which was odd because I thought you did a terrific job)!

Anyway, here's what I've been thinking: you need to stop worrying about pleasing people and just focus on pleasing Me. No, I'm serious! Don't worry so much about what people think of you—what you're wearing, what you look like, or even how talented you are. Are their opinions really the ones that matter most to you? Better pause to think about that!

Kids will be kids, and that means you'll get made fun of sometimes. When that happens, I'll be right here, ready to wipe away your tears and give you the courage to be yourself, no matter what. Because the truth is, it's My opinion that counts.

Next time you are tempted to worry about

what your friends think, stop and ask yourself, "Does it really matter?" All that matters is what I'm thinking, and I think you're pretty amazing.

♡ ♥ ♥ ♡ ♥ ♥

There are some who would like to lead you in the wrong way. They want to change the Good News about Christ. Even if we or an angel from heaven should preach another kind of good news to you that is not the one we preached, let him be cursed. As we said before, I will say it again. If any man is preaching another good news to you which is not the one you have received, let him be cursed. Do you think I am trying to get the favor of men, or of God? If I were still trying to please men, I would not be a servant owned by Christ. Christian brothers, I want you to know the Good News I preached to you was not made by man. I did not receive it from man. No one taught it to me. I received it from Jesus Christ as He showed it to me.

GALATIANS 1:7–12

The Things I Hate

Some people think that I *only* love and *never* hate. But (gasp!) here's the truth: there are some things I hate. (Are you shocked?) You'll find these things listed in today's verse, but let's talk this through.

I hate pride. (You know what pride is, right? It's when you think you're the best at everything.) And I can't stand hatred or murder. (Man, those things really get Me upset!) I'm also not happy when My kids lie about others or behave wickedly.

All of these things that I hate are bad. They're the opposite of how I want you to live. Instead of being prideful, build others up. Instead of lying, always tell the truth. Instead of behaving wickedly, be kind and considerate to others. Instead of hating. . .love.

In other words, please remove the things I hate from your life as much as you're able. Replace them with things like love, joy, peace, and hope.

I know what you're thinking. (No, seriously

. . .I really do.) You're saying, "What about my friends? They lie and cheat and behave badly too!" You're right. It's true. But guess what? You can hate sin and still love sinners. There will be a lot of people who lie to you or cheat you or hurt you in some way. It will take courage to go on loving, but you can do it, kiddo. After all, I keep loving you, even when you mess up.

A person of no worth, a sinful man, is he who goes about telling lies. He winks with his eyes, makes signs with his feet, and makes certain moves with his fingers. He always plans to do sinful things because of his sinful heart. He causes arguing among people. So trouble will come upon him all at once. Right then he will be broken, and there will be no healing. There are six things which the Lord hates, yes, seven that are hated by Him: A proud look, a lying tongue, and hands that kill those who are without guilt, a heart that makes sinful plans, feet that run fast to sin, a person who tells lies about someone else, and one who starts fights among brothers.

PROVERBS 6:12–19

Trapped!

You don't see what goes on outside while you're asleep, but I do! One night I saw a big raccoon knock over your trash can. That rascally little creature dug around inside the can and made a huge mess that your dad had to clean up the next morning. What a fiasco! Your dad is clever though! He set a trap to try to catch that raccoon. He put a cage out with the food inside and that raccoon fell for it! He ended up inside the cage not inside of the trash can.

In some ways sin is like that cage. When you sin, you get caught in a trap. Once you're in it. . . you're stuck! And stuck is no place to be!

I don't like My kids to be caught in traps. That's no way to live! It's impossible to get out without My help, just like it's impossible for that raccoon to get out of the cage without your father's help.

I never want you to be trapped in sin. My greatest desire is for you to be set free.

What sins have trapped you lately? Maybe it's time to make a list and ask for My help. (Hint: I already know what you're going to write down before you even write it.) I want the best for you, girlie, and that includes living a life of complete freedom!

So do not let sin have power over your body here on earth. You must not obey the body and let it do what it wants to do. Do not give any part of your body for sinful use. Instead, give yourself to God as a living person who has been raised from the dead. Give every part of your body to God to do what is right. Sin must not have power over you. You are not living by the Law. You have life because of God's loving-favor. What are we to do then? Are we to sin because we have God's loving-favor and are not living by the Law? No, not at all! Do you not know that when you give yourself as a servant to be owned by someone, that one becomes your owner? If you give yourself to sin, the end is death. If you give yourself to God, the end is being right with Him. At one time you were held by the power of sin. But now you obey with all your heart the teaching that was given to you. Thank God for this!
ROMANS 6:12–17

The Cares of Life

Some people count sheep to go to sleep. Other people fret and worry and have a hard time dozing off. They have too much on their minds to sleep.

I know you get like that sometimes, girlie. I remember that one night you were so worried about the test you had to take the next day. You tossed and turned all night! When you woke up the next morning you felt awful. You even begged your mom to stay home, but she wouldn't let you. And I remember that other time when you were so upset about the girls at school making fun of you that you barely slept a wink. Instead, you tried to figure out how you could fix the situation.

Here's the truth: worrying gets you nowhere. I'm not a fan of it, because it's the opposite of trust, which is what you really need to be doing. Besides, nighttime was created for resting, and how can you rest if you're upset?

It's going to take courage, but you've got to let go of those nighttime worries. Imagine I'm standing right in front of you. You take all of your worries and hand them to Me. I take them and carry them for you so you don't have to. And when you wake up in the morning, you suddenly feel great!

Rest easy, kiddo. I've got everything under control. So say your prayers and go to sleep.

"I tell you this: Do not worry about your life. Do not worry about what you are going to eat and drink. Do not worry about what you are going to wear. Is not life more important than food? Is not the body more important than clothes? Look at the birds in the sky. They do not plant seeds. They do not gather grain. They do not put grain into a building to keep. Yet your Father in heaven feeds them! Are you not more important than the birds? Which of you can make himself a little taller by worrying? Why should you worry about clothes? Think how the flowers grow. They do not work or make cloth. But I tell you that Solomon in all his greatness was not dressed as well as one of these flowers."

MATTHEW 6:25–29

This Is a Test

Pop quiz!

What goes through your mind when you hear those words? Likely, your heart starts beating fast, and you say to yourself, "Oh no! I haven't studied! I don't know what's going to be covered on the test!" You wonder how the teacher could be so mean, to surprise you with a test you weren't expecting.

Life is full of pop quizzes, tests that come unexpectedly. You've failed some, for sure, but you've passed lots more.

Here are a few examples. Remember that time your brother broke your favorite toy? You didn't exactly make a high score on that test when you threw the toy at him. You did much better the time your parents were going through a financial struggle. You remembered to pray in faith, and their finances got better. That's not the only time you impressed Me. Remember that time you went to your grandmother's house to help her tidy up? You worked without complaining. In fact, you ended up spending the whole day with her, and she loved every minute. Girl, you passed that test with flying colors.

You'll face challenges/tests every day of your life. It takes courage to look the test in the eye and say, "I'm going to beat you!"

When you face the test head-on and beat it, you're proving you've got faith (and that's important, trust Me). I don't ever want you to give up, no matter how hard the test might be.

♡ 🖤 🖤 ♡ 🖤 🖤

My Christian brothers, you should be happy when you have all kinds of tests. You know these prove your faith. It helps you not to give up. Learn well how to wait so you will be strong and complete and in need of nothing. If you do not have wisdom, ask God for it. He is always ready to give it to you and will never say you are wrong for asking. You must have faith as you ask Him. You must not doubt. Anyone who doubts is like a wave which is pushed around by the sea. Such a man will get nothing from the Lord. The man who has two ways of thinking changes in everything he does.

JAMES 1:2–8

You Needed a Savior

I've already shared the story about how I died for you and took away all of your sins. For My followers that was a sad, sad day. They still weren't 100 percent sure I was coming back to life. . .but I knew the truth. I knew I'd be back to join them once again, to prove that I really was who I said I was.

Still, what I had to go through that day was the hardest thing I've ever had to do—carrying that heavy cross up the hill, going through the physical pain of being hung on the cross. It was unbearable. But when I looked out at the crowd of people, guess who I saw?

You.

I saw you. I knew that you would one day be born and would need a Savior, someone to wash away all the bad things you've done. So I decided I would be as brave as I could and withstand the pain because I love you and want to give you this amazing gift.

I love having you as My kid, by the way. I've been thinking of you for ages, long before you were born, and you mean the world to Me. So learn from My example. Do the hard things. Be brave and courageous. You can do it, kiddo. I know you can.

Jesus carried His own cross to a hill called the Place of the Skull. There they nailed Him to the cross. With Him were two others. There was one on each side of Jesus. Then Pilate put a writing on the cross which said, JESUS OF NAZARETH, THE KING OF THE JEWS. This was read by many of the Jews. The place where Jesus was nailed to the cross was near the city. The writing was written in the Hebrew and the Latin and the Greek languages. Then the head religious leaders of the Jews said to Pilate, "Do not write, 'The King of the Jews'! Write, 'He said, I am the King of the Jews.'" Pilate said, "What I have written is to stay just as it is!"
JOHN 19:17–22

Never Too Young for Courage

People of every age need courage. You needed it when you were a baby. I remember how scared you were the first time you took a step toward your mama. You also needed it when you were a preschooler. (Remember that time you fell and skinned your knee?) You definitely need it in school, when bullies are picking on you or you're struggling to make it through an assignment you don't like.

The truth is, courage is a necessary requirement, even when you get to be an old woman. (Oh, I know. . .you can't imagine you'll ever be old. But one day you will be!) As you move from elementary age to junior high, much courage is needed. Some kids in this age group aren't so kind, but I hope you'll be one of the nice ones. And when you get to high school you'll need loads of courage just to figure out how to make it from one part of the school to the other! And don't even get Me started on college, marriage, and kids. Just trust Me when I say you're going to need oodles of courage.

Here's a promise from Me to you: I'll be right there, every step of the way. There's nothing you'll go through that I won't see. There! Doesn't that make you feel better?

Light is pleasing. It is good for the eyes to see the sun. If a man should live many years, let him have joy in them all. Yet let him remember the days of darkness, for they will be many. All that comes is for nothing. Young man, be filled with joy while you are young. And let your heart be happy while you are a young man. Follow the ways of your heart and the desires of your eyes. But know that God will judge you for all these things. So put away trouble from your heart, and put away pain from your body. Because the years when you were a child and the best years of your life are going by fast.

ECCLESIASTES 11:7–10

Courage to Pray

Remember that time you got really upset at your mom? You were so mad you couldn't think straight. (I remember it because Mom was praying hard that you would calm down and behave.) You got *so* angry that you didn't even think about praying, which really concerned Me. Instead, you just started throwing a temper tantrum instead. The madder you got, the worse things got. By the end of it all, Mom grounded you to your room and took away your video games. You were not happy about that one!

Here's a little secret, kiddo: on days like that when you're sitting all alone in your room, thinking about what happened. . .talk to Me. I won't get upset that you're angry, I promise. But I have to agree with Mom that things are better when you take a deep breath and chill!

I have a few hints for how you can calm down so we can have a good conversation. First, take a deep breath. Count to five. Blow it out and count to five. Then do that all over again. After a few deep breaths you'll be calm, cool, and collected.

Then tell Me what's going on in your heart. This will take courage, I know. Sometimes you don't like to talk about what you're really feeling, but I promise I can handle it.

I want you to be okay, sweet girl. I really do. Remember, I'm always here for you—even when you're mad.

Be full of joy always because you belong to the Lord. Again I say, be full of joy! Let all people see how gentle you are. The Lord is coming again soon. Do not worry. Learn to pray about everything. Give thanks to God as you ask Him for what you need. The peace of God is much greater than the human mind can understand. This peace will keep your hearts and minds through Christ Jesus. Christian brothers, keep your minds thinking about whatever is true, whatever is respected, whatever is right, whatever is pure, whatever can be loved, and whatever is well thought of. If there is anything good and worth giving thanks for, think about these things.

PHILIPPIANS 4:4–8

The Greatness of My Love

Love is powerful. In fact, it's the most powerful force on the planet! Love can heal relationships. Love can cause a person to stop doing bad things. Love can draw people to Me, even the ones with the hardest hearts.

I talk to you a lot about love, sweet girl, because it's so important. I'm not sure you understand just how important it is. If you want to know where true power, true courage comes from, you'll find it when you fall deeper in love with Me.

When you're filled with love for Me (and can sense My deep love for you), anything is possible! As today's scripture says, My love goes beyond anything you can understand. And when you're filled to the tippy-top, you'll overflow and spill that love onto the people around you.

I want you to understand how wide My love is. It's higher than any airplane in the sky! I want you to see how deep it is. Even the ocean floor isn't as deep. And wow, is My love ever powerful! Because of My love, I can offer you forgiveness. That means that nothing you can do or say will ever cause Me to stop loving you.

Today it's My greatest wish that you would fall deeper and deeper in love with Me, your Savior.

For this reason, I bow my knees and pray to the Father. It is from Him that every family in heaven and on earth has its name. I pray that because of the riches of His shining-greatness, He will make you strong with power in your hearts through the Holy Spirit. I pray that Christ may live in your hearts by faith. I pray that you will be filled with love. I pray that you will be able to understand how wide and how long and how high and how deep His love is. I pray that you will know the love of Christ. His love goes beyond anything we can understand. I pray that you will be filled with God Himself. God is able to do much more than we ask or think through His power working in us. May we see His shining-greatness in the church. May all people in all time honor Christ Jesus. Let it be so.

Ephesians 3:14–21

One Body, Different People

Have you ever wondered why I created so many different kinds of people? All across the planet you'll see people of every shape, size, and color. That's why I love the song "Jesus Loves Me" so much, because "red and yellow, black and white," they really are precious in My sight!

I love the little children in Africa. I adore the ones in Australia too. I'm crazy about the kiddos in North and South America, and I have a blast watching the ones who live in Asia and Europe. All across this great globe are children I care about, and I don't give one thought to what they look like or the color of their skin. I celebrate their differences, and so should you. In My eyes, they are all equally as lovable.

It takes courage to love all people equally. Some people believe they are more special because of the color of their skin or how pretty they are, but that's simply not true. All people are beautiful in My sight.

And since we're talking about it, you're beautiful too. Oh, I know—you look in the mirror and see freckles or a chubby tummy or legs that are too long and skinny. You groan and wish you could look like the other girls. I didn't make you like the other girls, honey! You are you. . .for a reason. So while you're treating others with respect, treat yourself that way too!

God has given me His loving-favor.
This helps me write these things to you.
I ask each one of you not to think more
of himself than he should think. Instead,
think in the right way toward yourself by the
faith God has given you. Our bodies are
made up of many parts. None of these parts
have the same use. There are many people who
belong to Christ. And yet, we are one body
which is Christ's. We are all different but we
depend on each other. We all have different
gifts that God has given to us by His loving-
favor. We are to use them. If someone has the
gift of preaching the Good News, he should
preach. He should use the faith God has given
him. If someone has the gift of helping others,
then he should help. If someone has the gift
of teaching, he should teach.

ROMANS 12:3–7

Dressed in My Armor

Imagine this: you're a soldier in the army. It's time to fight the enemy—but you're not wearing battle gear. You've got nothing to protect yourself. You're just wearing a T-shirt, shorts, and no shoes at all. *Ouch!*

Going into battle without the proper gear would be silly, wouldn't it? A real soldier would have a uniform, a helmet, and a weapon to protect himself. He would never think of facing down the enemy without his protective gear. The same is true of a police officer. What if she went out without her protective vest or her weapon? She wouldn't stand a very good chance against the bad guys!

I've given you armor, much like a soldier or a police officer would wear. I've given you a breastplate of righteousness, a helmet of salvation, the sword of the Spirit, and much, much more. I didn't give you all of this stuff to weigh you down. It's a gift to keep you safe when the enemy tries to harm you. When you put it on, you're taking on My strength, and My courage.

The enemy fights dirty, by the way! He'll

get you when you least expect it. But if you're wearing the proper armor, you'll do just fine. And don't ever forget, I'll be the one fighting through you, and My battle record is the best.

This is the last thing I want to say: Be strong with the Lord's strength. Put on the things God gives you to fight with. Then you will not fall into the traps of the devil. Our fight is not with people. It is against the leaders and the powers and the spirits of darkness in this world. It is against the demon world that works in the heavens. Because of this, put on all the things God gives you to fight with. Then you will be able to stand in that sinful day. When it is all over, you will still be standing. So stand up and do not be moved. Wear a belt of truth around your body. Wear a piece of iron over your chest which is being right with God. Wear shoes on your feet which are the Good News of peace. Most important of all, you need a covering of faith in front of you. This is to put out the fire-arrows of the devil. The covering for your head is that you have been saved from the punishment of sin. Take the sword of the Spirit which is the Word of God.
EPHESIANS 6:10–17

Trust...No Matter What

Do you trust Me? Sometimes I wonder. I see you trust in so many other things, but do you really, truly trust in Me?

Here's a fun test: Walk over to a light switch. Before you flip it, ask yourself, "When I do this, will the light really come on?" If the answer is yes, then you trust in the light switch. Your dad trusts that when he turns the key in his car, it will turn on. And guess what? Your mom is absolutely sure that if she mixes together eggs, butter, sugar, flour, and baking powder, she can bake a delicious cake.

To trust means you truly believe something will happen. You have no doubts, even when things don't seem to be going your way. You just keep hoping and believing. And I know you, kid. You want to be all of that.

Read My Word and you'll see that you really can trust in Me. My words are 100 percent true. If I said it, I will do it. That means you can safely put your faith in Me, no matter what.

Now I'm not saying it's always going to be

easy. You'll go through stuff that's stinkin' hard! But even in the valleys, when you're scared to death, you can ask for My courage to believe for the impossible. I'm a God of the impossible, after all! So, you can always trust in Me, in good times and bad.

My son, do not forget my teaching. Let your heart keep my words. For they will add to you many days and years of life and peace. Do not let kindness and truth leave you. Tie them around your neck. Write them upon your heart. So you will find favor and good understanding in the eyes of God and man. Trust in the Lord with all your heart, and do not trust in your own understanding. Agree with Him in all your ways, and He will make your paths straight. Do not be wise in your own eyes. Fear the Lord and turn away from what is sinful. It will be healing to your body and medicine to your bones.

PROVERBS 3:1–8

Friendships

I see you sitting there on the swing, all alone. You're watching the girls on the other side of the playground and wondering why they don't want to spend time with you. Your heart is hurting a little bit because one of them used to be your friend and now she's hanging out with other people, not you. You tried to reconnect with her, but she wasn't interested. Weird. You used to be so close. Now you're confused and feeling kind of lonely, and I don't blame you. It's hard when kids do this to each other.

I know what it feels like to be left out, sweet girl. I've had lots of people turn away from Me too. Boy, does it hurt My heart when they do. So I get it. You're in a hard spot, and it doesn't make any sense.

Still, I want you to know something. I have special friendships already planned for you. Look around the whole playground. See that girl sitting by herself on the bench? She's in need of a friend. And see that boy? You know the one. . . the other kids usually make fun of him because of how he dresses or acts. You could be a terrific friend to him.

You'll never know what a difference you can make until you try. So get brave! It will take plenty of courage to step out into new friend-ships, but let Me take care of that part. I'll give you all the courage you need, I promise.

God has chosen you. You are holy and loved by Him. Because of this, your new life should be full of loving-pity. You should be kind to others and have no pride. Be gentle and be willing to wait for others. Try to understand other peo-ple. Forgive each other. If you have something against someone, forgive him. That is the way the Lord forgave you. And to all these things, you must add love. Love holds everything and everybody together and makes all these good things perfect. Let the peace of Christ have power over your hearts. You were chosen as a part of His body. Always be thankful. Let the teaching of Christ and His words keep on living in you. These make your lives rich and full of wisdom. Keep on teaching and helping each other. Sing the Songs of David and the church songs and the songs of heaven with hearts full of thanks to God. Whatever you say or do, do it in the name of the Lord Jesus. Give thanks to God the Father through the Lord Jesus.

Colossians 3:12–17

My Ways Are Higher

Have you ever worked a hard puzzle that you just couldn't finish? Or maybe your teacher shared a riddle with the class and no matter how hard you tried, you simply couldn't figure it out. It was over your head.

That's kind of how it is when you try to figure Me out. If you try your entire life you will never truly get it. Your human mind can never comprehend all that I am. But that's okay! I don't ask you to know all things. I only ask that you have the courage to put your trust in Me.

Stop for a minute and think about the most amazingly brilliant person you know. I'm ten million times more brilliant than that. (I'm not bragging, by the way! I'm just telling it like it is!) Think about the most powerful bodybuilder you know. I'm a zillion times stronger.

I think about things that you can't even imagine. (And trust Me. . .I know you have an overactive imagination!) I perform miracles that you could never even describe. (And the way you tell stories is over-the-top fantastic!) I love in a way that is deeper and wider than any love you will ever experience.

The more you spend time with Me in prayer and Bible study, the more you will see that I want to share all of this with you, My child. Don't you feel special, that the Creator of the universe would take the time to think about you? Oh, but I do. That's because I adore you.

Look for the Lord while He may be found.
Call upon Him while He is near. Let the
sinful turn from his way, and the one who
does not know God turn from his thoughts.
Let him turn to the Lord, and He will have
loving-pity on him. Let him turn to our God,
for He will for sure forgive all his sins.
"For My thoughts are not your thoughts,
and My ways are not your ways," says the Lord.
"For as the heavens are higher than the earth,
so are My ways higher than your ways,
and My thoughts than your thoughts."
ISAIAH 55:6–9

How Children Must Live

I know what you're thinking. No, really. . .I do! You're trying to figure out why I make such a big deal out of kids obeying their parents. You're telling yourself, "It's too hard. I don't want to do it!" Sometimes you're even thinking that Mom and Dad don't deserve your good behavior because they don't pay enough attention to you. I would disagree.

So why do I care so much about obedience? Why do I want My girls to obey their parents, grandparents, teachers, and so on? Well, let's think about that for a minute. Imagine you're the parent. You tell your child to make her bed or clean her room. She doesn't. You tell yourself, "Okay, I'll just let it go. No big deal." Then a week later your child's room is a pigsty. It's filled with dirty clothes, stinky socks, dishes, and other icky things. Gross, right? At this point, it's making the whole house stink! You end up cleaning up her mess, but then she turns right around and messes it up again, not even caring. Unfair, right?

Your parents give you rules for your own

good. (I know, it doesn't always feel like it, but they do!) It's not easy, but trust Me with this, kiddo. Obeying your parents is a sign that you love Me. When you do what they ask, you're setting an example of that love, so. . .let it flow, girl!

Children, as Christians, obey your
parents. This is the right thing to do.
Respect your father and mother. This is
the first Law given that had a promise.
The promise is this: If you respect your father
and mother, you will live a long time and your
life will be full of many good things. Fathers,
do not be too hard on your children so they
will become angry. Teach them in their
growing years with Christian teaching.
Ephesians 6:1–4

Your Safe Place

Wiggly worms, spiders, snakes. . .life is filled with scary things! But don't you worry, girl! I'm your safe place. You can come to Me when you're feeling afraid. There's no point in pretending you're not.

I see you tossing and turning at night because you're scared of the dark. I also see you when you've got to stand up in front of your class to read your assignment. Your knees are knocking, and you're sweating like crazy. You get freaked out and convince yourself you can't do it. You would rather stay home from school and tell Mom you have a stomachache!

Oh, but you *can* do it, kiddo! With My help, you can do all things! That's a promise from Me to you.

Remember, I'm here to calm your fears. No matter what's going on in the world or what's happening in your own family, I'm your safe place. Give your fears to Me. It's simple! Just pray and tell Me what you're afraid of, then ask Me to take care of those worries for you. In that very moment, before you can say, "Please, Lord!" I've already done it. I've taken those worries from you and replaced them with faith.

Whew! Doesn't that feel good?

The Lord is my Shepherd. I will have everything
I need. He lets me rest in fields of green
grass. He leads me beside the quiet waters.
He makes me strong again. He leads me in the
way of living right with Himself which brings
honor to His name. Yes, even if I walk through
the valley of the shadow of death, I will not be
afraid of anything, because You are with me.
You have a walking stick with which to guide
and one with which to help. These comfort
me. You are making a table of food ready for
me in front of those who hate me. You have
poured oil on my head. I have everything I
need. For sure, You will give me goodness and
loving-kindness all the days of my life. Then I
will live with You in Your house forever.

PSALM 23:1–6

Focus on Others

One of the things I love most about you is how excited you get about stuff. That time Mom helped you redecorate your room? What a blast you had! And that other time when your parents planned a trip to a water park? You counted down the days in anticipation.

You can look forward to lots of things in life, and it's exciting to enjoy yourself, but don't get so excited that you forget about the needs of others. They need things to look forward to as well.

Think about it this way: your grandmother is lonely and needs something to get excited about. Maybe you could plan a visit! That little girl down the street, the one no one plays with. . .she needs something to get excited about too. Maybe you could invite her for a sleepover or offer to go to the park with her.

It's going to take courage to think about the needs of others more than your own, but I know you, sweet girl. You'll do it. Start by asking your parents what they're looking forward to. Maybe you could ask your teacher or principal too. I think it's time to take your eyes off of your own adventures and spend some time getting excited with others.

Are you strong because you belong to Christ? Does His love comfort you? Do you have joy by being as one in sharing the Holy Spirit? Do you have loving-kindness and pity for each other? Then give me true joy by thinking the same thoughts. Keep having the same love. Be as one in thoughts and actions. Nothing should be done because of pride or thinking about yourself. Think of other people as more important than yourself. Do not always be thinking about your own plans only. Be happy to know what other people are doing.

PHILIPPIANS 2:1–4

Don't Act Like the World

Sometimes I wish you could see things the way I see—from up in heaven. Girl, I see everything, and not all of it is good! Some kids (even the ones who say they're Christians) act crazy at times! It's kind of shocking, to be honest. They're disobedient to their parents, rude to their teachers, and mean to other kids. They lie, they cheat, they even steal! It's like they don't think the rules apply to them. Boy, are they wrong!

I'm going to ask you something hard today, something that's going to take a lot of courage on your part: please don't act like those people. It's possible to be different, and that's what I want you to be. No matter who makes fun of you, have the courage to be the kind of kid I want you to be.

When you asked Me to be your Savior and I came to live in your heart, I made everything new. Absolutely everything changed, including your thoughts. Now that your thoughts have become more like Mine, it's time to start listening more closely to what I say. Reading your Bible is more important than ever! After a while, you won't be like the kids who act up anymore. . .and that's a very good thing.

Christian brothers, I ask you from my heart to give your bodies to God because of His loving-kindness to us. Let your bodies be a living and holy gift given to God. He is pleased with this kind of gift. This is the true worship that you should give Him. Do not act like the sinful people of the world. Let God change your life. First of all, let Him give you a new mind. Then you will know what God wants you to do. And the things you do will be good and pleasing and perfect. God has given me His loving-favor. This helps me write these things to you. I ask each one of you not to think more of himself than he should think. Instead, think in the right way toward yourself by the faith God has given you.

ROMANS 12:1–3

Head over All

Imagine you are the queen of a make-believe land. All of your people have to obey the laws you set. (That part sounds like a lot of fun, right? Can you think of some laws you would pass right away?) You guard over your people carefully, making sure they obey you. You're very strict, making sure everyone follows your rules. But who do *you* obey? Who is your leader if you're the queen?

Now imagine you're the president of the United States. (Hey, it's possible! You could become president one day!) As president, you have a lot of power, don't you? You get to help pass laws and tell other people how to live. It's exciting to have that kind of power. But who tells *you* how to live?

All of the people of the world have to answer to Me, sweet girl. I'm the ultimate authority figure! I am the ruler over all rulers. (That means what I say goes!) I'm the King of all kings. (That means no one's more important than Me.) Every human being has to bow to Me, even the really important ones like kings and queens. I am the head of them all. And in Me, everyone is complete.

♡❤❤♡❤❤

*Be careful that no one changes your
mind and faith by much learning and
big sounding ideas. Those things are what
men dream up. They are always trying to
make new religions. These leave out Christ.
For Christ is not only God-like, He is God in
human flesh. When you have Christ, you are
complete. He is the head over all leaders and
powers. When you became a Christian, you
were set free from the sinful things of the
world. This was not done by human hands.
You were set free from the sins of your old
self by what was done in Christ's body.*

COLOSSIANS 2:8–11

Wait...and Get Stronger

Most of My kids aren't very patient. They want what they want and they want it *now*. Today, if possible! And boy oh boy, do some make a fuss if they don't get their way! I make sure they have the things they need in the proper time, of course, but some kids can get *so* demanding when I make them wait. They always want everything on their timetable, not Mine. If only they could understand that I have a bigger plan and My timing is perfect!

What about you, kiddo? Would you consider yourself to be patient or impatient? If you knew you were going to win first place at the school talent show, would you wait patiently until the day or would you wish, wish, wish it would happen right now, at this very minute?

Waiting is one of the hardest things you'll ever have to do. It takes courage, especially if you're waiting for something big! But if you'll wait on Me, I promise everything will work out for your good. And you'll get stronger and stronger as time goes on. The longer you have to wait, the more powerful you get.

When you think of it like that, then waiting is a good thing. I'll teach you things while you're being patient and grow you into a strong young lady.

While you're waiting, practice these words: "I'm getting stronger with time!" It's true, girl!

Have you not known? Have you not heard? The God Who lives forever is the Lord, the One Who made the ends of the earth. He will not become weak or tired. His understanding is too great for us to begin to know. He gives strength to the weak. And He gives power to him who has little strength. Even very young men get tired and become weak and strong young men trip and fall. But they who wait upon the Lord will get new strength. They will rise up with wings like eagles. They will run and not get tired. They will walk and not become weak.

Isaiah 40:28–31

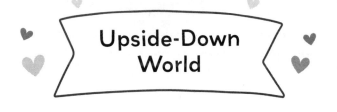

Upside-Down World

Wow, things are changing fast down there. Lots of people are up to no good! They're running around doing their own thing, following their own rules, and expecting others to follow after them.

If you ask them, things that used to be wrong are now right. And things that used to be right are now wrong. It's like they're making up their own rules! It's pretty clear to Me that lots of people have stopped reading My Word. If they would just read My story, they would see that I haven't changed. If I said it. . .I still mean it.

So how do you go about living right-side-up in an upside-down, inside-out world? Do you go along with the crowd? Do you do what they say? If they suddenly start saying that a lie is the truth or the truth is a lie, do you change just to match up with them?

The answer is no, girl. Don't go along with the crowd, especially if they're saying things that don't match up with what you know to be true! You keep reading your Bible. You keep doing what you know to be right in your heart. It's going to take courage (and you might be ridiculed), but don't give in to the temptation to think like the world. I can tell you, the world hardly ever gets it right!

You must understand that in the last days there will come times of much trouble. People will love themselves and money. They will have pride and tell of all the things they have done. They will speak against God. Children and young people will not obey their parents. People will not be thankful and they will not be holy. They will not love each other. No one can get along with them. They will tell lies about others. They will not be able to keep from doing things they know they should not do. They will be wild and want to beat and hurt those who are good. They will not stay true to their friends. They will act without thinking. They will think too much of themselves. They will love fun instead of loving God. They will do things to make it look as if they are Christians. But they will not receive the power that is for a Christian. Keep away from such people.
2 TIMOTHY 3:1–5

Don't Give In!

Maybe you've heard the word *temptation*. It means you want something you know you shouldn't have. Like when you're tempted to eat a second bowl of ice cream or you're tempted to disobey your parents.

I know you've been tempted to do the wrong thing at times. I could give you some examples of times you fell right into the temptation pit if you like. But I won't, because I know you see those times too. And besides, I've already forgiven you for those things.

I'm extra proud of you for the times you *don't* give in to temptation. And I want you to grow from the times you do give in and regret it.

Remember that time your mom bought a big bag of candy? She put it in the back of the pantry and said, "Don't touch this!" What did you want, more than anything else in the world? A piece of that candy, of course! In some ways, the temptations of life are like those sugary treats. You want them so badly, but you know you shouldn't eat them all because you'll end up with a bellyache.

Here's the solution to temptations: pray and ask Me to help. I know your weakness, and I'll step right in, helping you! Sure, it will take courage to do the right thing, but I know you, sweet girl. You're getting better and better at doing what's right.

Jesus came with them to a place called Gethsemane. He said to them, "You sit here while I go over there to pray." He took Peter and the two sons of Zebedee with Him. He began to have much sorrow and a heavy heart. Then He said to them, "My soul is very sad. My soul is so full of sorrow I am ready to die. You stay here and watch with Me." He went on a little farther and got down with His face on the ground. He prayed, "My Father, if it can be done, take away what is before Me. Even so, not what I want but what You want." Then He came to the followers and found them sleeping. He said to Peter, "Were you not able to watch with Me one hour? Watch and pray so that you will not be tempted. Man's spirit is willing, but the body does not have the power to do it."
MATTHEW 26:36–41

Stronger Hope

Wishing and hoping is kind of your thing, isn't it, sweetie? You're always wishing or hoping for something. Like that time you wished your parents would take you to Disney World. You knew they didn't have the money, but that didn't stop you from hoping!

And what about that time you were hoping for an A on that big math test? You knew the chances were slim, but that didn't stop you from hoping you could pull it off.

Hope is a wonderful gift that I give all of My kids. It's like a Christmas present wrapped in ribbons and bows. Hope is just what you need when you're feeling down in the dumps. It can lift your spirits in a hurry.

Hope isn't something you come up with on your own. You only get it if you put your trust in Me. I pour hope down on you like rain tumbling from the clouds in the sky. The more you ask for, the more I'll send!

Hope brings peace. Hope brings joy. Hope keeps you from worry, worry, worrying all the time. (And I know you, kid. You like to worry.)

Here's one more fun fact: your hope can g-r-o-w. It's true! You know how your feet are always growing? You change shoe sizes all the time. Well, hope is like that. When you put your trust in Me, the size of your hope gets bigger, bigger, and bigger!

Doesn't it feel good to have hope?

Our hope comes from God. May He fill you with joy and peace because of your trust in Him. May your hope grow stronger by the power of the Holy Spirit. I am sure you are wise in all things and full of much good. You are able to help and teach each other. I have written to you with strong words about some things. I have written so you would remember. God helped me write like this. I am able to write these things because God made me a missionary to the people who are not Jews. I work as a servant of Jesus Christ. I preach the Good News of God so the people who are not Jews may be as a gift to God. The Holy Spirit will set them apart so God will be pleased with them.
ROMANS 15:13–16

Butterflies in Your Tummy

I see how it is, kiddo. Sometimes when your teacher calls on you or when you have to get up in front of a crowd to speak, you get really scared. Your hands shake, and you get this weird fluttering sensation in your stomach. It's like you've got butterflies in there just flying around. They feel like they're having an argument or something. You wish they would take a hike so that you can get through the task in front of you, but it takes some time for those crazy butterflies to calm down.

Whenever you feel them fluttering in your tummy, it usually means you're about to have to do something you're terrified to do. But sweet girl, remember—I'm here to make you brave. I can calm those butterflies with just a word!

You might dread those butterflies because they make you feel even more nervous, but go ahead and do the hard things, even if you get that squishy, nervous feeling in your tummy. You're up for an adventure! Your butterflies may not show up very often, but when you do feel them, take a deep breath. Be brave. I'll give you courage in that very moment. Together we'll do the hard thing and that tummy will settle right down.

♡ ♥ ♥ ♡ ♥ ♥

"I have told you these things while I am still with you. The Helper is the Holy Spirit. The Father will send Him in My place. He will teach you everything and help you remember everything I have told you. Peace I leave with you. My peace I give to you. I do not give peace to you as the world gives. Do not let your hearts be troubled or afraid. You heard Me say that I am going away. But I am coming back to you. If you love Me, you would be glad that I am going to the Father. The Father is greater than I. I have told you this before it happens. Then when it does happen, you will believe."
JOHN 14:25–29

Sharp Friends

Your friends make you better, sweet girl. I know that they get on your nerves sometimes. They think they're funny when they're really not. And sometimes they poke fun at you or tease you. But mostly they're a blast to be around, aren't they? They "get" you in ways that strangers don't. That's because they know you so well.

Do you want to know what I think about godly friends? I think they make you sharper. No, I'm not saying you need to walk around with a pointy head like a pencil! I mean, they make you a better person.

Back in the old days, people would sharpen their knives or swords just by rubbing them together, iron against iron. Your godly friendships are a lot like that. When you hang out with friends who love Me (and love you), they make you better and you make them better. That's a win-win situation!

How do you make them better? By loving them. By saying, "Great job!" after they've done something well. By hugging them when they are sad. By saying good things about them behind their backs.

Today, decide to be a "sharp" friend, one who blesses and encourages those you love. I'll be clapping with joy as I see you both grow stronger and stronger in your faith.

A brother who has been hurt in his spirit
is harder to be won than a strong city, and
arguing is like the iron gates of a king's house.
A man's stomach will be filled with the fruit
of his mouth. He will be filled with what his lips
speak. Death and life are in the power of the
tongue, and those who love it will eat its fruit.
He who finds a wife finds a good thing, and
gets favor from the Lord. The poor man asks
for loving-kindness, but the rich man is hard
in his answers. A man who has friends must
be a friend, but there is a friend who
stays nearer than a brother.
PROVERBS 18:19–24

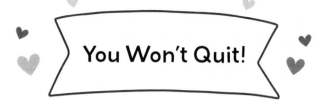

You Won't Quit!

You know what it's like to give up. You've done it a time or two.

For example, you're studying for a big test, but you don't feel like it. So you quit studying and play a video game. Then you wonder why your test grade isn't the best. Or maybe your mom tells you to clean your room. You start, but you don't finish. You get distracted looking at a toy or video game. (I've seen you do this, by the way, so there's no point in denying it!)

It's easy to get distracted, especially with so many temptations all around you. I get it. But, girl, I want you to keep going, even when you don't feel like it. (Hint: You won't always feel like it. Some days you'll feel just the opposite!)

Take a look at today's Bible verse. In this story, a woman refused to give up. Someone had wronged her, and she wanted the judge to pay attention to her case. It took awhile, but her persistence paid off. The judge finally ruled in her favor. It happened because she never gave up.

Finishing what you start is so important, especially when it comes to your walk with Me. You can't say, "Sure, Jesus! I'll follow You!" and then give up. I want you to keep your faith in Me forever, not just when you feel like it.

Finish what you've started, kiddo. It's how I want you to live!

Jesus told them a picture-story to show that men should always pray and not give up. He said, "There was a man in one of the cities who was head of the court. His work was to say if a person was guilty or not. This man was not afraid of God. He did not respect any man. In that city there was a woman whose husband had died. She kept coming to him and saying, 'Help me! There is someone who is working against me.' For awhile he would not help her. Then he began to think, 'I am not afraid of God and I do not respect any man. But I will see that this woman whose husband has died gets her rights because I get tired of her coming all the time.'" Then the Lord said, "Listen to the words of the sinful man who is head of the court. Will not God make the things that are right come to His chosen people who cry day and night to Him? Will He wait a long time to help them? I tell you, He will be quick to help them. But when the Son of Man comes, will He find faith on the earth?"

LUKE 18:1–8

White as Snow

Remember that time you played outside in the rain? Before long, you were a muddy mess. You didn't even care in the moment. You just kept splishing and splashing until every part of you was covered in icky-slicky, gooey mud. You even soaked your clothes, and Mom had to work extra-hard to get them clean.

That's kind of what it's like when you come to know Me for the very first time. You show up looking a little, well, dirty. It's like you're covered head to toe in mud. And, like your Mom, I've got to clean you up. But My way of doing it is a little different. Instead of sticking you in the bathtub (not that I have anything against baths) I just forgive you and all of that dirtiness is washed away in an instant! I won't scold or fuss either. I'll just look at you and say, "Here, sweet girl. . .let Me get you spic-and-span!"

How does a "Jesus cleanup" work, you want to know? When I died on the cross, My blood washed away all of your sins. You just have to believe in your heart that I died for you and ask

Me to come and live in your life. Make Me your Lord and Savior. Then you are fully clean, white as snow. No more mud on you, girl!

Christ was before all things. All things are held together by Him. Christ is the head of the church which is His body. He is the beginning of all things. He is the first to be raised from the dead. He is to have first place in everything. God the Father was pleased to have everything made perfect by Christ, His Son. Everything in heaven and on earth can come to God because of Christ's death on the cross. Christ's blood has made peace. At one time you were strangers to God and your minds were at war with Him. Your thoughts and actions were wrong. But Christ has brought you back to God by His death on the cross. In this way, Christ can bring you to God, holy and pure and without blame. This is for you if you keep the faith. You must not change from what you believe now. You must not leave the hope of the Good News you received. The Good News was preached to you and to all the world. And I, Paul, am one of Christ's missionaries.
COLOSSIANS 1:17–23

Stop the Gossip Train

"All aboard the gossip train!" That's what your friends say, anyway. "Come sit by me and tell me everything! I want to know all of the such-and-such about so-and-so! Don't leave out one juicy detail! Spill the tea, girl!"

Trust Me, gossip really is like a train barreling down the tracks. The story travels from one person to the next to the next. It just keeps going until everyone has heard the news. Gossip. . . gossip. . .mumble. . .mumble! On and on the story goes, twisting and changing over time, until the person who's being gossiped about could really get hurt by what's being said.

Can I tell you something, kiddo? I'm not a fan of gossip. I don't like it at all. It hurts people and destroys confidences. You know what that feels like, I know. You've been gossiped about in the past, and it hurts.

But you have also participated in gossip, and that needs to stop. Get off that train, girlie! Take a look at today's verse. See that part where it says you should live without blame? That's not just about lying and cheating. It's about gossiping too.

Have a little talk with your ears. Tell them, "You're closed to gossip! You'll hear it no more."

♡ ♥ ♥ ♡ ♥ ♥

I will be careful to live a life without blame. When will You come to me? I will walk within my house with a right and good heart. I will set no sinful thing in front of my eyes. I hate the work of those who are not faithful. It will not get hold of me. A sinful heart will be far from me. I will have nothing to do with sin. I will stop whoever talks against his neighbor in secret. I will not listen to anyone who has a proud look and a proud heart. My eyes will look with favor on the faithful in the land, so they may serve me. He who walks without blame will help me. He whose ways are false will not live in my house. He who tells lies will not stand in front of me. I will destroy all the sinful in the land every morning. I will cut off all those who do wrong from the city of the Lord.

PSALM 101:2–8

The Courage to Forgive

I'm not a fan of bullying or hurting others. It really upsets Me when people push others around or say horrible things to them. It bothers Me when they gang up on people, and I'm especially upset when they get into fights!

It should bother you too. It's so unfair for a whole group of people to pick on one person. Lots of people enjoy hurting others, and I think it needs to stop. Those bullies injure innocent people with their words, and sometimes they hurt them with their actions too. The really bad ones use their fists and end up getting into trouble! (Some grown-up bullies end up in jail.)

It takes courage to deal with meanies. If you know someone who's a bully, speak up! Tell a teacher. Tell your parents. Don't keep the news to yourself because someone could really get hurt.

By the way, there is one thing that's even harder than watching bullies do their thing. And that's finding the courage to forgive them when they repent. It might seem impossible, but that's what I'm asking you to do. It doesn't mean you have to be their friend, but go ahead and forgive the people who've hurt you, even the ones who bullied and made fun of you. I promise, you'll feel better when you do.

Forgiveness is never easy, especially when you're dealing with people who've truly hurt you. Remember, I am your hope and trust. I will protect you. And I will help you bravely begin to forgive others for the wrong things they say or do.

I have a safe place in you, O Lord. Let me never be ashamed. Because You are right and good, take me out of trouble. Turn Your ear to me and save me. Be a rock to me where I live, where I may always come and where I will be safe. For You are my rock and my safe place. O my God, take me from the hand of the sinful, from the hand of the wrong-doer and the man without pity. For You are my hope, O Lord God. You are my trust since I was young. You have kept me safe from birth. It was You Who watched over me from the day I was born. My praise is always of You. I have become a wonder and surprise to many. For You are my strong safe place. My mouth is filled with Your praise and with Your honor all day long.

Psalm 71:1–8

Be a Jesus Copycat

I know how much you like to play copycat. Your friend says something and you repeat her words back to her, just to be silly. Or maybe she wears a pink shirt to school one day so you decide to wear pink the next. It's fun, right?

Copycatting can be good or bad, depending on your heart. If you're making fun of the person—repeating the same words they just spoke—it's not good. In fact, that makes Me very sad. I can see that you're just making fun of them and trying to ridicule them. But if you're copying their behaviors or manners out of respect, then it is a good thing. Maybe you're learning manners from your big sister or learning how to clean the house from your mom.

Here's some fun news: copying Me is *always* a good thing. You're saying, "I want to be like You, Lord!"

So how can you copycat Me? Let your words be words of love, just like Mine. Treat others with respect. Pray for people who are sick or in trouble. Don't judge them. Make things easier on others. That's how I love.

Remember, follow the leader is a terrific game, as long as I'm the leader! I love it when you copy Me—in your behaviors, your speech, and your attitude.

My dear children, I am writing this to you so you will not sin. But if anyone does sin, there is One Who will go between him and the Father. He is Jesus Christ, the One Who is right with God. He paid for our sins with His own blood. He did not pay for ours only, but for the sins of the whole world. We can be sure that we know Him if we obey His teaching. Anyone who says, "I know Him," but does not obey His teaching is a liar. There is no truth in him. But whoever obeys His Word has the love of God made perfect in him. This is the way to know if you belong to Christ. The one who says he belongs to Christ should live the same kind of life Christ lived.

1 John 2:1–6

Helpers

I'm always on the lookout for helpers, people who are willing to help others. I've been watching, and I want you to know how proud I am when you stop to help others. Like that time you helped your mother unload the groceries from the car and put them away. Or that time you helped your teacher hand out papers in class. And what about that time you helped your grandmother sort through her old photos? These helping moments show Me that you're paying attention to the needs of others, and that's great!

Maybe when you grow up you'll still love to help others. If you do, here are some fun ideas: You might help out at a homeless shelter or provide food for a family in need. Maybe you'll help an elderly neighbor who needs a ride to the doctor. These little things aren't so little, you know. Any time you reach out a helping hand, I'm watching. . .and smiling.

It takes courage to help. Sometimes you'd rather not. You would prefer to watch a show on TV or play a video game. Maybe you'd rather take a nap. But if you follow through and help others in need, you will make My heart very, very happy.

Are you strong because you belong to Christ? Does His love comfort you? Do you have joy by being as one in sharing the Holy Spirit? Do you have loving-kindness and pity for each other? Then give me true joy by thinking the same thoughts. Keep having the same love. Be as one in thoughts and actions. Nothing should be done because of pride or thinking about yourself. Think of other people as more important than yourself. Do not always be thinking about your own plans only. Be happy to know what other people are doing.

PHILIPPIANS 2:1–4

Making Progress

Look at you, girl! You're really making progress! You wanted to become healthier, so you're sticking to a healthy eating plan. You wanted to make better grades, so you're studying more and paying attention in class. You want to have a better relationship with your mom and dad, and you're learning to speak to them with love and respect. (Can I just pause for a moment to tell you how happy it makes your parents when you do that? They've had a few chats with Me about your behavior in the past, and we're all happy to see you're shaping up.)

Every time you make a little more progress, I feel like throwing a party with you as the guest of honor! Can you hear Me applauding when you do the things you said you would do? I'm very excited (and impressed) that you're doing such a great job. But then again, I always knew you had it in you. You're destined for greatness, after all.

There will be times when you're tempted to give up. Please don't! When things get tough and it feels like you don't have the courage to keep going, just come to Me. Remember, I'm your safe place. You can confess anything to Me, and I'll just go on loving you. But I'll also show you what to do to get on track again. So stick with it, kiddo! I'm proud of that progress!

Turn away from the sinful things young people want to do. Go after what is right. Have a desire for faith and love and peace. Do this with those who pray to God from a clean heart. Let me say it again. Have nothing to do with foolish talk and those who want to argue. It can only lead to trouble. A servant owned by God must not make trouble. He must be kind to everyone. He must be able to teach. He must be willing to suffer when hurt for doing good. Be gentle when you try to teach those who are against what you say. God may change their hearts so they will turn to the truth. Then they will know they had been held in a trap by the devil to do what he wanted them to do. But now they are able to get out of it.
2 TIMOTHY 2:22–26

Choose to Serve Me

Not everyone in this world wants to follow Me. It's sad but true. Some people say I don't exist. Others believe I exist, but they don't want to live the kind of life I desire. So they do their own thing and live for themselves. They don't want to make My heart happy. They just want to make themselves happy. (Sounds a little selfish, right?)

You though? You're a girl who follows hard after Me. That means you want to be close to Me and to make Me proud. It means you keep going, even when you feel like giving up. I'm so proud of you, kiddo! You're making good choices and living a life that would make any father proud.

Even if everyone around you decides *not* to follow Me, you should still do it anyway. It makes My heart happy when you stand up for what you believe.

Read these verses from Joshua and you will see that I want you to choose to be on My team, no matter what. I want you to choose to serve Me even if no one else will. It takes courage to live like this. Will you be courageous and take a stand for Me even if others do not? Today, you get to choose.

"So fear the Lord. Serve Him in faith and truth. Put away the gods your fathers served on the other side of the river and in Egypt. Serve the Lord. If you think it is wrong to serve the Lord, choose today whom you will serve. Choose the gods your fathers worshiped on the other side of the river, or choose the gods of the Amorites in whose land you are living. But as for me and my family, we will serve the Lord." The people answered, "May it never be that we turn away from the Lord and serve other gods. For the Lord our God is the One Who brought us and our fathers out of the land of Egypt, from the house where we were made to work. He did these powerful works in front of our eyes. He kept us safe everywhere we went, among all the nations we passed through. The Lord drove away from in front of us all the nations, even the Amorites who lived in the land. So we will serve the Lord. For He is our God."

Joshua 24:14–18

A Different Point of View

Imagine your mom says, "Hey, we're going out to eat. Where do you guys want to go?"

Your kid brother might want pizza. You might want a burger and french fries. Your parents might want to eat a steak and baked potato. (Is all of this food-talk making you hungry?) Everyone has their own opinion. But in the end you compromise and go along with the group. It just makes things easier if you don't squabble about what you want when you're together.

Compromise is good when you're with your parents, but it's not always good when you're hanging out with your friends. Like when they want you to lie to the teacher or be mean to that girl on the playground that no one really talks to. In those moments, it's better *not* to compromise or to go along with the crowd.

I know you, girlie. You want to please everyone and don't like to quarrel, so you keep quiet sometimes instead of speaking up. But I want you to courageously speak the truth when they try to get you to go along with them. Don't compromise what you know to be true. Have your own opinion. Stick with it.

And remember, being different isn't a bad thing! It's better to be one-of-a-kind than to follow after the group. That's what pleases My heart, after all.

I did not give up waiting for the Lord. And He turned to me and heard my cry. He brought me up out of the hole of danger, out of the mud and clay. He set my feet on a rock, making my feet sure. He put a new song in my mouth, a song of praise to our God. Many will see and fear and will put their trust in the Lord. How happy is the man who has made the Lord his trust, and has not turned to the proud or to the followers of lies. O Lord my God, many are the great works You have done, and Your thoughts toward us. No one can compare with You! If I were to speak and tell of them, there would be too many to number.

PSALM 40:1–5

The Faith of Stephen

Have you read the story of Stephen? You'll find it in Acts chapter 7. But you'd better prepare yourself before you read. This is a tough one, girl.

Stephen loved Me. He was one of My biggest fans. He loved Me so much that he wanted to tell more and more people about all I had done for him. He was a true missionary at heart!

Not everyone wanted to hear what he had to say though. Stephen was arrested for sharing his story and found guilty by the judge! He was given the death sentence. (Can you even imagine? What if telling others about Me was punishable by death? Would you still share the good news?)

Even as he was about to be put to death, Stephen was full of My Spirit. He looked up. And when he did, do you know what he saw? He saw Me, standing at the right hand of My Father, God. That gave him all the courage he needed.

I want you to learn from Stephen's journey. No matter what you go through, you can be brave. You can have the faith of Stephen if you look up (even in the middle of the crisis). I'm right there. . .and I care about what you're going through. You can trust Me, even when everything around you appears to be crumbling. Don't *give* up. Just *look* up.

The Jews and religious leaders listened to Stephen. Then they became angry and began to grind their teeth at him. He was filled with the Holy Spirit. As he looked up to heaven, he saw the shining-greatness of God and Jesus standing at the right side of God. He said, "See! I see heaven open and the Son of Man standing at the right side of God!" They cried out with loud voices. They put their hands over their ears and they all pushed on him. Then they took him out of the city and threw stones at him. The men who were throwing the stones laid their coats down in front of a young man named Saul. While they threw stones at Stephen, he prayed, "Lord Jesus, receive my spirit." After that he fell on his knees and cried out with a loud voice, "Lord, do not hold this sin against them." When he had said this, he died.
ACTS 7:54–60

A Babble of Voices

I know you like to go to parties! I've watched you celebrate at birthdays with friends and family members. Parties can be loud and crazy! Sometimes you're surrounded by noise on every side. That can make it tough to have a heart-to-heart conversation with a friend with all those people yap-yap-yapping!

That's how it is in life too. Sometimes you try so hard to hear My voice, but all the other voices are getting in the way. Your friends, TV, video games, even social media. . .it's just hard to focus on Me when so many things are babbling, babbling, babbling. Man, they're loud! Whew!

All these clamoring voices can be frustrating during hard times. If you want to watch Me work a real miracle, you've got to pull away and spend quiet time with Me. Sweet girl, that's what I want most of all, to hang out with you! During our quiet times together I'll give you courage, I'll build your faith, and I'll help you solve those problems you're so worried about. But you've

got to quiet those other voices so you can hear
Me loud and clear.

*"For sure, I tell you, the man who goes
into the sheep-pen some other way than
through the door is one who steals and
robs. The shepherd of the sheep goes in
through the door. The one who watches the
door opens it for him. The sheep listen to the
voice of the shepherd. He calls his own sheep
by name and he leads them out. When the
shepherd walks ahead of them, they follow
him because they know his voice. They will not
follow someone they do not know because they
do not know his voice. They will run away from
him." Jesus told this picture-story to them.
Yet they did not understand what He said.*
JOHN 10:1–6

Using Your Gifts

Imagine it's Christmas morning. (Yay! Best day of the year!) It's time to open the presents under the tree. One of them is an amazing bike, the very one you've been hoping for! It's pink and white and has tassels hanging from the handlebars. There's even a place to store your water bottle while you ride.

You can't believe it! Your parents gave you exactly what you'd hoped for! (They were paying attention to all those hints you were dropping.) You want to ride it right away, of course. No one can get you off of it. Up and down the street you go, showing off your new gift.

Then after a few weeks, you get bored with it and stop riding it. Months later you see that it has a flat tire, but you don't really care because you don't ride it anyway. Then a couple of years later you notice cobwebs on it. Wow! You really need to ride that bike, don't you? But getting back on it doesn't sound as exciting as it once did.

The same is true with the gifts I've given you. Whether you sing, act, dance, or memorize scripture for the Bible quiz, I hope that every single gift will be used for Me, not just now but for years to come. Don't let them get covered in cobwebs, girl! Start using those gifts today.

What are some God-given gifts you need to start using again?

Loving-favor has been given to each one of us. We can see how great it is by the gift of Christ. The Holy Writings say, "When Christ went up to heaven, He took those who were held with Him. He gave gifts to men." When they say, "He went up," what does it mean but that He had first gone down to the deep parts of the earth? Christ Who went down into the deep also went up far above the heavens. He did this to fill all the world with Himself. Christ gave gifts to men. He gave to some the gift to be missionaries, some to be preachers, others to be preachers who go from town to town. He gave others the gift to be church leaders and teachers. These gifts help His people work well for Him. And then the church which is the body of Christ will be made strong.

EPHESIANS 4:7–12

A Long March

Have you ever wondered why I commanded Joshua to march around the city of Jericho for seven days before I knocked the walls down? I could've done it in an instant after all. But I wanted to check out Joshua's obedience to see if he would pass the test.

The truth is, I like to involve My kids in the story. I could perform miracle after miracle, sure, but it's better if you're part of that miracle!

Oh, I know. . .you don't always want to participate. Sometimes you wish I'd just show up and take care of all the hard stuff for you. (Boy, wouldn't that make things easier?!) But I want your participation. Instead of letting your worries get to you, step out in faith. Play the role you need to play. Do the thing you need to do. And then when I *do* bring those walls down, you'll be able to look back on the situation and say, "I never gave up!" You can also say, "My faith sure grew a lot during that trial."

I promise to show up, just like I did for Joshua. I promise to knock those walls down. But I can't wait to see the role you're going to play in the story, girl. It's going to be a doozy! So keep your faith every step of the way and grow, grow, grow!

"Be strong and have strength of heart. For you will bring the people in to take this land which I promised to their fathers to give them. Only be strong and have much strength of heart. Be careful to obey all the Law which My servant Moses told you. Do not turn from it to the right or to the left. Then all will go well with you everywhere you go. This book of the Law must not leave your mouth. Think about it day and night, so you may be careful to do all that is written in it. Then all will go well with you. You will receive many good things. Have I not told you? Be strong and have strength of heart! Do not be afraid or lose faith. For the Lord your God is with you anywhere you go."

JOSHUA 1:6–9

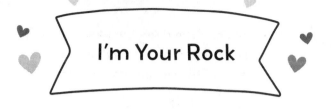

I'm Your Rock

Why do you suppose My Word (the Bible) calls Me your rock? Maybe it's because a rock (at least a big one like a boulder) doesn't move. The storms come, and the rock just sits there. Winds blow, and it doesn't tumble down the hill. The rock is secure in its place. It's faithful. You can count on it.

I'm just like that, kiddo! I'm solid like a rock! You can count on Me. And here's another fun fact: I will never change. The words that I spoke in the Bible are as true today as they were thousands of years ago.

Best of all, I'm not going anywhere—not ever. I'll never leave you or forsake you. (That's a promise.) People all around you might disappear. Some will move away. Others simply don't want to be friends anymore. But like that rock, I won't move. I'm in your life to stay.

A rock is strong—some are so strong that they can't be moved. And I'm the strongest of the strong. What no one else can do. . .I can do. And here's some cool news: I still perform miracles. I still heal the sick. I still answer prayers. In other words, I still care.

Yep, I'm your rock. You can count on Me no matter what!

I love You, O Lord, my strength. The Lord is my rock, and my safe place, and the One Who takes me out of trouble. My God is my rock, in Whom I am safe. He is my safe-covering, my saving strength, and my strong tower. I call to the Lord, Who has the right to be praised. And I am saved from those who hate me. The ropes of death were all around me. The floods of death make me afraid. The ropes of the grave were all around me. The traps of death were set for me. I called to the Lord in my trouble. I cried to God for help. He heard my voice from His holy house. My cry for help came into His ears.

PSALM 18:1–6

A Very Special Lunch

I want to share a story about a very special lunch I had with some friends. I was teaching on a hillside and thousands of people were there listening to Me. After a while they all got hungry.

My disciples were worried. They thought the people would be upset if we didn't offer them food. One little boy was willing to share his lunch of five loaves of bread and two fish.

Now, I had My work cut out for Me! I had to multiply those five loaves of bread and two little fish to feed over five thousand people! As you might recall, I'm pretty good with miracles. This was the perfect opportunity to show everyone that I was in the miracle-working business.

Everyone watched as I prayed over the food . . .and it multiplied! No matter how much food the disciples passed out, there was always plenty more. Some people thought it was some sort of magic trick, but it wasn't.

I provided what was needed on that amazing day, and I'm still in the "providing" business. You don't need to worry and fret when you're facing a crisis like the one the disciples faced that day. I've already got the answer. I'll meet your need, wait and see! And you'll be right there, watching and trusting just like that boy with the sack lunch.

Today, place your trust and hope in Me. Don't be afraid to believe for a miracle!

When it was evening, His followers came to Him. They said, "This is a desert. The day is past. Send the people away so they may go into the towns and buy food for themselves." Jesus said to them, "They do not have to go away. Give them something to eat." They said to Him, "We have only five loaves of bread and two fish." Jesus said, "Bring them to Me." He told the people to sit down on the grass. Then He took the five loaves of bread and two fish. He looked up to heaven and gave thanks. He broke the loaves in pieces and gave them to His followers. The followers gave them to the people. They all ate and were filled. They picked up twelve baskets full of pieces of bread and fish after the people were finished eating. About five thousand men ate. Women and children ate also.

MATTHEW 14:15–21

Courage to End Friendships

Let's talk about your friendships. Now you and I both know that some of your friends are amazing. They're wonderful, godly girls. Some of the others though? They're really struggling. A few of them are doing things they shouldn't (even though they know what they're doing is wrong). You're doing your best to be a good friend, but sometimes (just keeping it real) you get caught up in their drama and end up doing the wrong thing.

Reality check, kiddo—I want you to be a good witness to these girls, but at the same time I don't want you pulled into their trap. Some friendships become toxic (like poison) when things get out of hand. Like when that friend tries to get you to do things you know you shouldn't.

Here's what I want you to do when that happens: if you find yourself stuck with friends who you know aren't the right ones to have, you will need a lot of courage to break off those bad friendships and find some good friends. But don't worry. . .I will help you.

You might end up feeling lonely. Or your old, not-so-great friends might say bad things about you. Even when it hurts, I promise you'll be happy when you choose to stop hanging out with the wrong crowd.

♡ 🖤 🖤 ♡ 🖤 🖤

I ask you, Christian brothers, watch out for those who make trouble and start fights. Keep your eye on those who work against the teaching you received. Keep away from them. Men like that are not working for our Lord Jesus Christ. They are chained to their own desires. With soft words they say things people want to hear. People are fooled by them. Everyone knows you have obeyed the teaching you received. I am happy with you because of this. But I want you to be wise about good things and pure about sinful things. God, Who is our peace, will soon crush Satan under your feet. May the loving-favor of our Lord Jesus be yours.
ROMANS 16:17–20

Twelve Words

It's not always easy to apologize, even if you know that what you did was wrong. It takes courage to look someone in the eye and say, "I messed up!" It's even harder if the person is really upset at you. But I want you to have the courage to apologize when you make mistakes, sweet girl. It's important because it takes away that guilty feeling.

Apologizing can also heal broken relationships. Maybe your friend isn't speaking to you right now because of something mean you did to her. Maybe you said something ugly about her behind her back and she found out. Ouch. It's time to make things right, kiddo. Perhaps if you go ahead and make things right, she'll be your friend again.

So how do you go about apologizing? It's not easy, but here are twelve words you can speak that will heal just about any broken relationship: "I am sorry. I was wrong. I love you. Please forgive me." You'll be stunned at how quickly I can use those twelve words to bring healing.

It's going to take courage, I know. But remember, I'm watching over you as you step out in faith and apologize. I'll soften the heart of the person you've hurt. Together we can mend what's been broken.

Go ahead. You can do it.

Put away the old person you used to be. Have nothing to do with your old sinful life. It was sinful because of being fooled into following bad desires. Let your minds and hearts be made new. You must become a new person and be God-like. Then you will be made right with God and have a true holy life. So stop lying to each other. Tell the truth to your neighbor. We all belong to the same body. If you are angry, do not let it become sin. Get over your anger before the day is finished. Do not let the devil start working in your life.

EPHESIANS 4:22–27

Second Chances

Remember that time Mom said, "I'm only giving you one chance to get this right!" You paid attention! You did what she told you to do, and I was so proud of you. (Mom was proud too, by the way. She's always happy when you listen to her and do what you're told.)

Not everyone gets it right the first time. They mess up and then hope for a second chance. I know you know what that feels like, because you've had a lot of second chances. Like that time your mother told you to clean your room . . .only you didn't. Or that time she told you to stop irritating your brother. . .and you couldn't seem to. Yep, you've made a few mistakes over the years. But you've learned your lessons!

It takes courage to try again when you've already failed once, but that's exactly what I want you to do—keep trying, no matter how long it takes. Try. . .and try. . .and try again. Just don't give up, okay? I want you to learn from your mistakes then do the right thing when you're given another opportunity.

You'll have plenty of second chances in life, kiddo, but I hope you don't need them. I hope you do your best to get things right the very first time.

This is what we heard Him tell us. We are passing it on to you. God is light. There is no darkness in Him. If we say we are joined together with Him but live in darkness, we are telling a lie. We are not living the truth. If we live in the light as He is in the light, we share what we have in God with each other. And the blood of Jesus Christ, His Son, makes our lives clean from all sin. If we say that we have no sin, we lie to ourselves and the truth is not in us. If we tell Him our sins, He is faithful and we can depend on Him to forgive us of our sins. He will make our lives clean from all sin. If we say we have not sinned, we make God a liar. And His Word is not in our hearts.

1 John 1:5–10

The Giant and the Little Boy

We already talked about David and Goliath. Remember? David was the small boy with a fist full of rocks who took down a mighty giant. Pretty impressive, right?

These "David and Goliath" stories happen all the time, even now. The big guy picks on the little guy. And the little guy hardly ever wins. (Let's face it. . .some of those giants are pretty big!)

David managed to take down his Goliath. He showed him once and for all that the little guys can win if I am on their side. Maybe you read that story and say, "That's great for David, but you don't know the giants I face! There's no way I could knock them down with five smooth stones."

Don't be so sure, girlie! Do you really think it was David's strength that knocked Goliath off his feet? No way! I placed My supernatural *Zap! Bang! Pow!* strength in that rock and it went flying. . .all the way across the field until it struck Goliath and he hit the ground!

Don't worry if your knees are knocking. Don't turn and run! Goliath won't take you down as long as you ask for My help. Be brave. Be strong. Stand up to him, and I'll make a way for you to win that battle. I am bigger and stronger than any giant. I've already breathed My power into you to knock those giants down! Get ready, girl!

The Philistine came near to David, with the man carrying his shield in front of him. When the Philistine looked and saw David, he thought nothing of him. For he was only a young man, with good color in his skin, and good-looking. The Philistine said to David, "Am I a dog, that you come to me with sticks?" And the Philistine spoke against David by his gods. The Philistine said to David, "Come to me. I will give your flesh to the birds of the sky and the animals of the field." Then David said to the Philistine, "You come to me with a sword and spears. But I come to you in the name of the Lord of All, the God of the armies of Israel, Whom you have stood against. This day the Lord will give you into my hands. I will knock you down and cut off your head. This day I will give the dead bodies of the army of the Philistines to the birds of the sky and the wild animals of the earth. Then all the earth may know that there is a God in Israel."

1 SAMUEL 17:41–46

Heroes of the Faith

Sometimes you think you're the only one who gets afraid, but that's not true. If you read My book, the Bible, you'll see that the great men and women mentioned in the Old and New Testaments all struggled with fear. That's right! The very people who are best known for their faith once struggled with fear and doubt.

Moses led the Israelites through the wilderness toward the Promised Land, but he wasn't sure he had what it took to be a good leader.

Mary (My mother) was nervous when the angel told her she was going to have a baby.

Elijah faced the prophets of Baal, but his hands were shaking!

Here's a cool fact. These amazing men and women became super-duper strong and brave because they refused to let fear win. They put their trust in Me. And you know what happens when you trust Me. . .I give you My strength. (Aren't you glad it's not up to you?)

I'm the one who saves you when you come up against an obstacle. I'm the same God who helped Abraham, Noah, David, Elijah, Moses, and even My mom. That means I can (and will) help you, just like I helped them. You can trust in Me. Don't be afraid. I'll be your strength. Just let Me work through you, kiddo!

All these many people who have had faith in God are around us like a cloud. Let us put every thing out of our lives that keeps us from doing what we should. Let us keep running in the race that God has planned for us. Let us keep looking to Jesus. Our faith comes from Him and He is the One Who makes it perfect. He did not give up when He had to suffer shame and die on a cross. He knew of the joy that would be His later. Now He is sitting at the right side of God. Sinful men spoke words of hate against Christ. He was willing to take such shame from sinners. Think of this so you will not get tired and give up.

HEBREWS 12:1–3

Led by the Spirit

Hey, kiddo! I want to tell you a story about something I went through when I first started My ministry. I went out into the desert to spend forty days fasting (going without food and water) to get My heart ready for ministry. I needed time to pray, to think, and to be with My Father, because I knew the work ahead of Me was going to be hard. While I was out there, the devil came to tempt Me. (Sound familiar? He tempted Adam and Eve too!) That slippery devil did all he could to torment Me and accuse Me of not being the Savior of the world, but I showed him! I wouldn't change My story, no matter what he said.

The devil loves to tempt people like that. He usually comes after you when you're feeling low, then he torments, pressures, and accuses. You're so tired you don't feel like fighting, so sometimes you let him win.

I don't want you to let him win, sweet girl. You've got more power in your pinkie finger than he has in all of his being! Take a close look at today's scripture. Notice a key phrase: *Jesus was led by the Spirit.* That's what saved Me in the desert, and My Spirit will save you too. The voice of the enemy will still ring out, but you don't need to worry about that. My Spirit will give you courage and guide you through!

Jesus was full of the Holy Spirit when He returned from the Jordan River. Then He was led by the Holy Spirit to a desert. He was tempted by the devil for forty days and He ate nothing during that time. After that He was hungry. The devil said to Him, "If You are the Son of God, tell this stone to be made into bread." Jesus said to him, "It is written, 'Man is not to live by bread alone.'" The devil took Jesus up on a high mountain. He had Jesus look at all the nations of the world at one time. The devil said to Jesus, "I will give You all this power and greatness. It has been given to me. I can give it to anyone I want to. If You will worship me, all this will be Yours." Jesus said to the devil, "Get behind Me, Satan! For it is written, 'You must worship the Lord your God. You must obey Him only.'"

LUKE 4:1–8

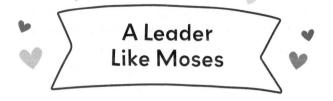

A Leader Like Moses

My people, the Israelites, lived as slaves in Egypt for many generations, but I had something bigger in store for them! I had prepared a land (Israel) just for them. Still, they had to get there, and it wasn't a short journey. It would take a lot of energy to plan a trip for that many people. (Have you ever tried to go on a vacation with a large group? It's not easy!)

When the time came for them to leave Egypt and head to the Promised Land, I knew they needed a good, strong leader. So I chose a man named Moses. Now Moses was like many of My kids. He didn't think he was the best leader. In fact, he was pretty sure he would be the worst possible leader. "I have a problem with my speech!" he said. "I stutter!" He argued with Me and said, "I'm not up for the job. Pick someone else, please!" But I didn't let him get away with that. I had big plans for Moses. He led his people through the desert to the land I had prepared for them, and he did it in My strength.

Can you relate to Moses? Have you ever thought, *I'm not right for this job! The teacher needs to pick someone else.* The truth is, you can do all things through Me because I'll give you My strength. Like Moses, you can do amazing things, far beyond what you even imagine. Don't give up before you start, girl!

Moses said to the Lord, "Lord, I am not a man of words. I have never been. Even now since You spoke to Your servant, I still am not. For I am slow in talking and it is difficult for me to speak." Then the Lord said to him, "Who has made man's mouth? Who makes a man not able to speak or hear? Who makes one blind or able to see? Is it not I, the Lord? So go now. And I will be with your mouth. I will teach you what to say." But Moses said, "O Lord, I ask of You, send some other person." Then the anger of the Lord burned against Moses. He said, "Is not Aaron the Levite your brother? I know he can speak well. Also, he is coming to meet you. And when he sees you, he will be glad in his heart. You must speak to him and put the words in his mouth. I will be with your mouth and his mouth. I will teach you what you are to do. He will speak to the people for you. He will be a mouth for you. And you will be as God to him."

EXODUS 4:10–16

The Breath of My Spirit

I see how it is, sweet girl. Some days you feel super-duper strong, like you could win every battle! Other days, not so much. But you know what? Even on the hard days, when you're just not feeling it, you can be strong through Me. With one breath of My Spirit I can give you supernatural energy to get the job done!

Think of it like this. It's a perfectly calm day with no winds blowing. Then all of a sudden, a tornado blows through! It's so powerful that it knocks things down! That's how it is when you're filled with My Spirit. You're like a spiritual tornado filled with power that can change the landscape around you! No, you won't knock down buildings. But you will pray for the sick and watch them get better. You'll work up the courage to share your faith with friends. . .and they will come to know Me. You'll be able to stand up to the bullies and not back down.

How are you feeling today? On a scale of one to ten, where's your strength? If you're at a two, no worries! I can turn things around in a hurry. If you're at a nine, awesome! Head out the door and do great things for Me!

As they were gathered together with Him,
He told them, "Do not leave Jerusalem.
Wait for what the Father has promised.
You heard Me speak of this. For John the
Baptist baptized with water but in a few days
you will be baptized with the Holy Spirit."
Those who were with Him asked, "Lord, is this
the time for You to give the nation back to the
Jews?" He said, "It is not for you to know the
special days or the special times which the
Father has put in His own power. But you will
receive power when the Holy Spirit comes into
your life. You will tell about Me in the city of
Jerusalem and over all the countries of Judea
and Samaria and to the ends of the earth."

Acts 1:4–8

Forgive Yourself

You've forgiven your friend for that time she hurt your feelings. You've forgiven your parents for that time they paid more attention to your little sister than to you. You've even forgiven your teacher for giving you that pop quiz. But why can't you seem to forgive yourself?

I don't like it when My kids beat themselves up over things they've done in the past. It's not easy to let go. I get that. But once you've asked for My forgiveness, I give it. . .right then and there! That naughty thing you did? It's gone. And I hope you'll let go of it too. There's no point in holding on to the disappointment or the pain. Those mean words you spoke to your mother when she asked you to put the dishes in the sink? As soon as you asked for My forgiveness, I washed your bad deeds away. I even reminded you to apologize to Mom for saying those ugly words. Thanks for following through on that, by the way.

Have the courage to forgive yourself, sweet girl. Stop beating yourself up over things from the past. Let go of the things that make you feel guilty. They've been washed away, like water under a bridge.

So from now on, we do not think about what people are like by looking at them. We even thought about Christ that way one time. But we do not think of Him that way anymore. For if a man belongs to Christ, he is a new person. The old life is gone. New life has begun. All this comes from God. He is the One Who brought us to Himself when we hated Him. He did this through Christ. Then He gave us the work of bringing others to Him. God was in Christ. He was working through Christ to bring the whole world back to Himself. God no longer held men's sins against them. And He gave us the work of telling and showing men this. We are Christ's missionaries. God is speaking to you through us. We are speaking for Christ and we ask you from our hearts to turn from your sins and come to God.

2 Corinthians 5:16–20

An Obedient Walk

Have you ever tried to walk a large, energetic dog? It's not always easy, especially when the dog is bigger than you are! Sometimes that feisty pooch ends up walking you, not the other way around! It's not fun to be pulled around, is it? And it's dangerous for the dog too. What if he got loose and ended up getting hit by a car?

It's hard to get a dog under control, but I'll tell you a little secret. . .sometimes it's hard to get you under control too. You're almost as rowdy as Fido sometimes! You want to take off running, leaving Me behind. You've got places to go, people to see, and you forget that I'm the One who needs to be leading the way.

It breaks My heart when you take off without Me. I've got amazing things for you to do, but you need to stick close to Me, sweet girl. When you take steps alongside Me, you'll be safe. And when you encounter scary things, I'll be right there to give you courage. Best of all, I'll be whispering things like, "Do this; don't do that!" so you know what to do at all times.

Don't pull on the leash, girl! Let Me have the reins and I promise you'll have the best journey of your life.

The way of the man who is right with God is smooth. O Upright One, make the path straight of those who are right with You. While following in Your ways, O Lord, we have waited for You. To remember You and Your name is the desire of our souls. My soul has a desire for You in the night. Yes, my spirit within me looks for You in the morning. For when you punish the earth, the people of the world learn what is right and good. When favor is shown to the sinful, he does not learn what is right and good. He goes on doing what is wrong in the land of those who are right. He does not see the wonderful power of the Lord.
ISAIAH 26:7–10

Practically Perfect in Every Way?

What if I told you that I want you to live a blameless life? What would you think? No doubt you would say, "Jesus wants me to be perfect? I'll never come close!"

Nope. I don't expect perfection, though it's nice to watch you *try* to do the right things. I just want you to do your best, make the finest choices, and stick close to Me, so I can help you when you get off-track.

You won't get it right all the time. (Sorry, but it's the truth! You'll blow it sometimes. All of My kids do.) There are going to be days when you mess up big-time, and you might even wonder if I can make things right again.

Oh, but I can! I'm right here, ready to forgive and help you get it right. And guess what? When I forgive you it washes that sin away. Right then, in that very instant. Before you can even say, "I promise not to do it again!" I've already taken care of it. And here's another bit of good news: I don't even remember it anymore. So in the blink of an eye you really are perfect in My sight, not because of what you've done but because of what I've done.

♡ ♥ ♥ ♡ ♥ ♥

O Lord, who may live in Your tent?
Who may live on Your holy hill? He who
walks without blame and does what is right
and good, and speaks the truth in his heart.
He does not hurt others with his tongue,
or do wrong to his neighbor, or bring shame
to his friend. He looks down upon a sinful
person, but honors those who fear the Lord.
He keeps his promises even if it may hurt
him. He gives money to be used without being
paid for its use. And he does not take money
to hurt those who are not guilty. He who does
these things will never be shaken.

PSALM 15:1–5

How Forgiveness Works

I love to hear from you when things are going great and even when they're not. Sometimes you mess up—make a big mistake—and you stop talking to Me. That makes Me so sad! I especially want to hear from you when you need My forgiveness and help.

I know, I know. . .some people say, "God will forgive me, no matter what." They don't even feel the need to ask. But I have to share something with you, sweet girl—I like to hear you say, "I messed up. I'm sorry. Please forgive me." Those words warm My heart.

When you confess your sin (you admit you did it and you're sorry you did it, not just sorry you got caught), I'm faithful and just to forgive. You'll feel so much better when you get things off your chest, for sure.

Today, take a look at your life, especially things you've done that you regret. Have you admitted them to Me? Are you truly sorry? If so, then I will gladly forgive you for those sins, and you never ever have to worry about them again.

You can totally forget that they ever happened. Whew! Doesn't that feel better?

♡ ♥ ♥ ♡ ♥ ♥

This is what we heard Him tell us. We are passing it on to you. God is light. There is no darkness in Him. If we say we are joined together with Him but live in darkness, we are telling a lie. We are not living the truth. If we live in the light as He is in the light, we share what we have in God with each other. And the blood of Jesus Christ, His Son, makes our lives clean from all sin. If we say that we have no sin, we lie to ourselves and the truth is not in us. If we tell Him our sins, He is faithful and we can depend on Him to forgive us of our sins. He will make our lives clean from all sin. If we say we have not sinned, we make God a liar. And His Word is not in our hearts.

1 JOHN 1:5–10

The Courage to Do What's Right

I was watching the day your friend tried to pressure you into doing something you both knew was wrong. I could tell how icky you felt inside as you tried to figure out what to do. In spite of that feeling (which was a little nudge from My Spirit, by the way), you messed up. Worst of all, you knew what was right, but in that moment you made the wrong choice.

I could hear the thoughts going through your head: *Maybe it would be okay, just this once. Maybe I can get away with it.*

Forget about the maybes. It's *always* better to choose what's right.

There will be a million opportunities to do the wrong thing. You'll face temptations at school, at home, even at church! And trust Me when I say there will always be people who want to lead you down the wrong path.

Don't take the wrong road, sweet girl. I want to celebrate with you when you do the right thing! When you choose to do things My way, I promise I'll give you the courage to see them through. I won't leave you hanging (or humiliated).

Toughen up, girl! Be strong and courageous so you can make excellent choices that we can both be proud of.

♡ ♥ ♥ ♡ ♥ ♥

But He gives us more loving-favor.
For the Holy Writings say, "God works
against the proud but gives loving-favor to
those who have no pride." So give yourselves
to God. Stand against the devil and he will
run away from you. Come close to God and
He will come close to you. Wash your hands,
you sinners. Clean up your hearts, you who
want to follow the sinful ways of the world and
God at the same time. Be sorry for your sins
and cry because of them. Be sad and do not
laugh. Let your joy be turned to sorrow.
Let yourself be brought low before the Lord.
Then He will lift you up and help you.
JAMES 4:6–10

Learning from Nature

Isn't it lovely, to walk in the woods down a long, winding trail? There's so much to discover—caterpillars climbing up a tree, slithering lizards in the grass, even a baby deer shooting across the path, chasing his mother.

I created all of nature as a gift to you, My child. The green grass, the autumn leaves, tiny lizards, birds flying overhead. . .they're all for you! I want you to see them all, to enjoy watching over them, much as I enjoy watching over you.

You can learn so much from the creatures around you! From the caterpillar you can learn to keep working, working, working. . .until you finally turn into a butterfly. From the dog you can learn how to obey. From the birds you can learn how to soar above your circumstances. From the baby deer you can learn how to stay precious and sweet, and close to your parents.

I want you to trust Me as the animals trust Me. Have the same courage that a mama bird has when she pushes her baby out of the nest for the first time. Have the same joy that a hyena has when he's laughing. In other words, enjoy these precious gifts I've given you.

All of nature points to Me. Learn from My creation and grow.

"But ask the wild animals, and they will teach you. Ask the birds of the heavens, and let them tell you. Or speak to the earth, and let it teach you. Let the fish of the sea make it known to you. Who among all these does not know that the hand of the Lord has done this? In His hand is the life of every living thing and the breath of all men. Does not the ear test words as the mouth tastes food? Wisdom is with old men, and understanding with long life."
JOB 12:7–12

A Bright Future

I've got such big plans for you! Don't you wish you knew what I know? I know what you're going to be when you grow up, who you're going to marry, and how many kids you'll have. I even know where you'll live and what kind of job you'll have.

You don't know any of that yet. But that's part of the adventure. It's more fun not to know, and simply to trust Me. It'll be a fun adventure, I promise! I have little surprises all along your journey, things I will reveal when the time is right. Oh, how you'll love the special things I've got planned!

I know you worry sometimes about the future. You fret over things like how you'll do in school, where you'll go to college, and whether or not you'll go through some of the hard things your parents and grandparents have gone through.

This much I can reveal to you, sweetheart. I'm watching every moment of your life, and I'm going to take care of you. When hard times come (and they will. . .they come to everyone) I'll be close by, holding your hand.

Your future looks bright! So don't fret over

what you don't know. Just keep taking steps in the right direction and leave the rest to Me.

This is what the Lord says, Who makes a way through the sea and a path through the powerful waters, Who brings out the war-wagon and the horse, the army and the strong man, (They will lie down together and will not rise again. They are destroyed, put out like the fire of a little light): "Do not remember the things that have happened before. Do not think about the things of the past. See, I will do a new thing. It will begin happening now. Will you not know about it? I will even make a road in the wilderness, and rivers in the desert. The wild animals will honor Me, the wild dogs and the ostriches. For I give waters in the wilderness, and rivers in the desert, to give drink to My chosen people. The people whom I made for Myself will make known My praise."
Isaiah 43:16–21

Shake Off That Worry!

I see what's going on in that heart of yours. You've got a big test coming up, and you're scared. You don't think you'll pass it. You've studied and done all you can (and I'm so proud of you for that), but you're still worried.

Here's the problem with fretting over things like schoolwork, kiddo. Worry only steals your joy and your energy, which makes the problem even worse.

Let's say you've got a big project to turn in. You work on it, but you're not happy with the way it turns out. The night before it's due you toss and turn in bed, and when you wake up in the morning, you have a headache and feel icky all over. All from fretting.

In many ways worry is like a thief who shows up at your house, asking for you to let him in. Would you open the door to a burglar? I don't think so! You would slam that door shut and lock it right away, then push a piece of furniture up against it, just to be sure! In the same way, don't open your heart to worry, sweet girl. It's up to no good!

Trust Me, even with things like this. It will take courage to give these things to Me, but do it anyway. I promise you'll feel so much better if you take your hands off and give these worries to Me.

♡ 🖤 🖤 ♡ 🖤 🖤

"I tell you this: Do not worry about your life. Do not worry about what you are going to eat and drink. Do not worry about what you are going to wear. Is not life more important than food? Is not the body more important than clothes? Look at the birds in the sky. They do not plant seeds. They do not gather grain. They do not put grain into a building to keep. Yet your Father in heaven feeds them! Are you not more important than the birds? Which of you can make himself a little taller by worrying? Why should you worry about clothes? Think how the flowers grow. They do not work or make cloth. But I tell you that Solomon in all his greatness was not dressed as well as one of these flowers."
MATTHEW 6:25–29

All Things

Repeat these two words out loud: *All things.* Say them again: *All things.*

Today's verse says that you can do all things through Me.

Now, I know what you're thinking: "Me? I can do amazing, hard things?"

Yes. Yes, you can. Because I'll be the one doing them through you. I'll give you the strength to accomplish goal after goal. When you're facing a hard test in school and think you won't make it, I will give you strength. When you need to work up the courage to talk to that girl who's been making fun of you, I will strengthen you even then! When you finally get around to cleaning that messy closet, I'll help you through it. And when you're praying for someone in need (like a sick friend or a grandmother who needs healing), I'll be right there, giving you the strength to believe for a miracle.

Are you wondering why it's *My* strength, not yours? If you had to depend on yourself, you would panic. Even the strongest human being is weak compared to Me! So depend on My strength. Let Me do what you can't. When you step aside and let Me work, I really can do *all* things.

Christian brothers, keep your minds thinking about whatever is true, whatever is respected, whatever is right, whatever is pure, whatever can be loved, and whatever is well thought of. If there is anything good and worth giving thanks for, think about these things. Keep on doing all the things you learned and received and heard from me. Do the things you saw me do. Then the God Who gives peace will be with you. The Lord gives me a reason to be full of joy. It is because you are able to care for me again. I know you wanted to before but you did not have a way to help me. I am not saying I need anything. I have learned to be happy with whatever I have. I know how to get along with little and how to live when I have much. I have learned the secret of being happy at all times. If I am full of food and have all I need, I am happy. If I am hungry and need more, I am happy. I can do all things because Christ gives me the strength.
PHILIPPIANS 4:8–13

Three Hebrew Children

Have you ever felt like you were walking through the fire? Sometimes things get so heated up (with your parents, your friends, or your schoolwork) that you might feel that way!

No one understood what that felt like more than Shadrach, Meshach, and Abednego—the three Hebrew men who were thrown into a fiery furnace because they refused to bow down to the ungodly king. I was so proud of them for sticking up for what was right. (I'm proud of you when you do that too!) Those three guys marched bravely into the furnace, not knowing if they would live or die!

But they didn't die. I kept them safe. In fact, when they walked out of the flames their hair didn't even smell of smoke. (Impressive, right?) You can imagine how shocked the king was. He was terrified, because he realized in that moment that I had protected these three boys.

I'll do the same thing for you when you go through fiery trials. I'll protect you, I promise. I will bring you through it. Just look to Me and have courage when hard times come. I'll be right there, seeing you through. You'll make it through and won't even have the smell of smoke in your hair.

Then Nebuchadnezzar became very angry and called for Shadrach, Meshach, and Abed-nego. And they were brought to the king. Nebuchadnezzar said to them, "Is it true, Shadrach, Meshach and Abed-nego, that you do not serve my gods or worship the object of gold that I have set up? Now if you are ready to get down on your knees and worship the object I have made when you hear the sound of the horns and harps and all kinds of music, very well. But if you will not worship, you will be thrown at once into the fire. And what god is able to save you from my hands?" Shadrach, Meshach and Abed-nego answered and said to the king, "O Nebuchadnezzar, we do not need to give you an answer to this question. If we are thrown into the fire, our God Whom we serve is able to save us from it. And He will save us from your hand, O king. But even if He does not, we want you to know, O king, that we will not serve your gods or worship the object of gold that you have set up."

DANIEL 3:13–18

Walking on Water

I want to tell you a story of something that happened to Me once. My disciples were in a boat on the Sea of Galilee. I had remained behind on the land to pray. I decided to join them on the boat, and (much to their surprise) I walked across the water to get to them. Boy, were they shocked when I came strolling toward them!

Peter (one of the disciples who loved Me very much) decided to try walking on the water himself. He stepped out of the boat and did okay at first. But after a few seconds he took his eyes off of Me and started to sink. For a minute, it looked like he might drown! I called out, "Peter! Keep looking at Me and you'll do fine!" And, that's exactly what happened. When he kept his gaze on Me, he didn't sink. Whew!

I wanted to show My disciples that they can have faith and courage as long as they put their trust in Me, not themselves. I want you to learn that lesson too, kiddo. Whenever things get rough, don't look at your circumstances. Look at Me. Together, we'll perform miraculous feats if you'll just keep the faith.

♡ 🖤 ❤️ ♡ 🖤 ❤️

*Just before the light of day, Jesus went
to them walking on the water. When the
followers saw Him walking on the water,
they were afraid. They said, "It is a spirit."
They cried out with fear. At once Jesus spoke
to them and said, "Take hope. It is I. Do not be
afraid!" Peter said to Jesus, "If it is You, Lord,
tell me to come to You on the water." Jesus
said, "Come!" Peter got out of the boat and
walked on the water to Jesus. But when he saw
the strong wind, he was afraid. He began to
go down in the water. He cried out, "Lord, save
me!" At once Jesus put out His hand and took
hold of him. Jesus said to Peter, "You have so
little faith! Why did you doubt?" When Jesus
and Peter got into the boat, the wind stopped
blowing. Those in the boat worshiped Jesus.
They said, "For sure, You are the Son of God!"*

MATTHEW 14:25–33

How to Eat an Elephant

Have you ever heard the saying, "How do you eat an elephant? One bite at a time!"

It's true! (Not that I recommend eating elephants. That's not the point of this story.) When you have a big job to tackle—something really huge—you can't do it all at once. You have to take baby steps to reach your goal.

Let's say your dad decides he needs to lose twenty pounds. He goes on a diet and starts watching what he eats. He joins a gym and works out. He turns down your mother's famous chocolate pie. In other words, he does all the right things. Will he lose that whole twenty pounds in a day? Of course not! He's taking baby steps, one pound at a time until he reaches his goal, but every step is a step in the right direction.

You've got goals too. I see inside that heart of yours. You want to do well with that big project the teacher gave you. It's not due for a month, but you're already working on it a little at a time. Atta girl! Take baby steps toward your goals. I'll help you push away any fear or doubt. I'll give you the courage to keep taking steps, even when things don't go your way.

You'll eat this elephant, girlie. . .one bite at a time!

You know that only one person gets a crown for being in a race even if many people run. You must run so you will win the crown. Everyone who runs in a race does many things so his body will be strong. He does it to get a crown that will soon be worth nothing, but we work for a crown that will last forever. In the same way, I run straight for the place at the end of the race. I fight to win. I do not beat the air. I keep working over my body. I make it obey me. I do this because I am afraid that after I have preached the Good News to others, I myself might be put aside.
1 Corinthians 9:24–27

Courage to Believe

People don't always want to believe in Me, do they? It's especially hard when they ask you questions like, "Where is your God? I can't see Him."

They do have a point. It's hard to believe in what you can't see with your eyes or hear with your ears. That's why you've got to open your spiritual eyes and ears. You can't see Me with your earthly eyes, but you've seen Me work miracles in your life, so you know I'm right here. I've healed sick people that you know, taken care of your family when you were going through a hard time, and even helped you with your schoolwork.

Many times, I've revealed Myself to you through My actions. So if you ever doubt, just look back on how far you've come. Remember all of the many times I stepped in and fixed problems for you (or your family). You'll be reminded in a hurry that I really am who I say I am!

It's so great that you want all of your friends to know Me. Keep on sharing the things I've done for you and some of those boys and girls just might start believing. Maybe others won't, but don't be discouraged! I'm going to give you courage to go on believing, even when it's really hard. So trust Me, girl! Have courage! Keep believing, even if it doesn't make sense.

Martha said to Jesus, "Lord, if You had been here, my brother would not have died. I know even now God will give You whatever You ask." Jesus said to her, "Your brother will rise again." Martha said to Him, "I know that he will rise again when the dead are raised from the grave on the last day." Jesus said to her, "I am the One Who raises the dead and gives them life. Anyone who puts his trust in Me will live again, even if he dies. Anyone who lives and has put his trust in Me will never die. Do you believe this?" She answered, "Yes, Lord, I believe that You are the Christ, the Son of God. You are the One Who was to come into the world."

JOHN 11:21–27

You Need to Change!

"You need to change!" How do you feel when you hear those words? Probably a little nervous, right? Change. . .what? And how? And when?

Change is a part of life, and some changes are easier than others. But what about the times when Mom says, "Change your attitude, girl!" or "Change the way you talk to me. It's not respectful!" *Ouch.* It's not so easy to make those changes, is it?

Here's the thing, kiddo. I look at your life and I see areas that need a little—shall we say—adjustment. Your temper gets out of control sometimes. And remember that time you were tempted to sneak candy when Mom wasn't looking? You gave in to the temptation then lied about it when you got caught. That stuff's gotta go.

So what are the hardest things for you to change? (Maybe it's time to make a list.) Start with attitude. (I know, I know! You wish you didn't have to tackle that one. I understand, sweet girl!) Maybe a few other things need changing too. . . your grades, maybe. Or your eating habits. Or the way you treat your kid brother. I could make the list for you, but then you'd miss out of the fun of doing it yourself. So get to it!

It takes courage to admit that you need to change, but I know you. . .you can do it.

Christian brothers, do not talk against anyone or speak bad things about each other. If a person says bad things about his brother, he is speaking against him. And he will be speaking against God's Law. If you say the Law is wrong, and do not obey it, you are saying you are better than the Law. Only God can say what is right or wrong. He made the Law. He can save or put to death. How can we say if our brother is right or wrong? Listen! You who say, "Today or tomorrow we will go to this city and stay a year and make money." You do not know about tomorrow. What is your life? It is like fog. You see it and soon it is gone. What you should say is, "If the Lord wants us to, we will live and do this or that." But instead you are proud. You talk loud and big about your-selves. All such pride is sin. If you know what is right to do but you do not do it, you sin.

James 4:11–17

Cluck-Cluck-Clucking

Some people are nervous all the time. They're hard to be around because they never stop worrying, in good times and bad. They go on and on and on, telling you all of their problems. No matter how you try to make them feel better, they just keeping fretting. (Do you know that word? *Fretting* just means they're anxious and worried.)

In many ways, a fretter is like a hen that won't stop clucking. That fretful bird marches around the yard, digging, scratching, clucking . . .fretting. (Annoying, right?) She's not making any progress. All of her yapping solves nothing! But somehow all of the noise makes her feel better. She doesn't even care that she's bothering the neighbors! On and on she goes, cluck-cluck-clucking! She wears people out with her never-ending clucking. The complaining makes her feel a little better (for a moment), but before long she's down in the dumps again.

Don't be a clucker, girlie. Don't pace and scratch. Look at the verse from Proverbs 12:25. Fretting will just weigh you down. And you don't need that!

Look up, up, up! I've got the answer whenever you need courage. Speak words of faith over your situation. That clucking doesn't motivate Me one bit. I swing into action when I hear your praise and words of faith!

Be full of joy always because you belong to the Lord. Again I say, be full of joy! Let all people see how gentle you are. The Lord is coming again soon. Do not worry. Learn to pray about everything. Give thanks to God as you ask Him for what you need. The peace of God is much greater than the human mind can understand. This peace will keep your hearts and minds through Christ Jesus. Christian brothers, keep your minds thinking about whatever is true, whatever is respected, whatever is right, whatever is pure, whatever can be loved, and whatever is well thought of. If there is anything good and worth giving thanks for, think about these things. Keep on doing all the things you learned and received and heard from me. Do the things you saw me do. Then the God Who gives peace will be with you.

PHILIPPIANS 4:4–9

A Contest on the Mountain

Hey, girl! Do you know the story of Elijah? He was one of My prophets in Old Testament times, and what a mighty man he was! He had My power and strength inside of him, just like you do. I gave Elijah a fun idea—to challenge the prophets of Baal (a false god) to see which of us was the one true God. He instructed Baal's followers to build an altar and to lay a sacrificial bull on it. Then they were to call on their (false) god to light the altar on fire.

I wish you could've seen it! The false prophets begged and pleaded with their false god for hours, but absolutely nothing happened! Boy, were they bummed. But now it was time for Me to show off a little. Elijah prepared an altar of wood. He placed a bull on it and told the men to soak the whole thing in water three times. Then he called out to Me, the One True God, and guess what I did? I lit that altar on fire! Boy, was that a day to remember!

Here's why I'm telling you this: Elijah's knees were knocking (at least a little bit) when he called on Me. He almost lost his courage. But I came through for him, and I'll come through for you too!

♡ ♥ ♥ ♡ ♥ ♥

Then Elijah took twelve stones, by the number of the families of Jacob's sons. The word of the Lord had come to Jacob's sons, saying, "Israel will be your name." With the stones he built an altar in the name of the Lord. And he made a ditch around the altar, big enough to hold twenty-two jars of seed. Then he set the wood in place. He cut the bull in pieces and laid it on the wood. And he said, "Fill four jars with water and pour it on the burnt gift and on the wood." Then he said, "Do it a second time." And they did it a second time. He said, "Do it a third time." And they did it a third time. The water flowed around the altar, and filled the ditch also. Then the time came for giving the evening gift. Elijah the man who spoke for God came near and said, "O Lord, God of Abraham, Isaac and Israel, let it be known today that You are God in Israel. Let it be known that I am Your servant, and have done all these things at Your word. Answer me, O Lord. Answer me so these people may know that You, O Lord, are God. Turn their hearts to You again." Then the fire of the Lord fell. It burned up the burnt gift, the wood, the stones and the dust. And it picked up the water that was in the ditch.

1 Kings 18:31–38

The Future

I can see into the future. It's crazy to think about that, I know, but it's true! You don't have any idea what's going to happen five minutes from now, or even an hour from now. But I know.

I saw you before you were born (when you lived inside your mom), and I will see you all the way to the part where you join Me in heaven.

I know how many years you will live, whom you will marry, how many children you will have, what sort of things you will like to do. . .I literally know it all! I've got a big plan for your future— your talents, your abilities, the kind of job you'll have. . .everything!

Here's a big question: How do you feel about the fact that I know all of that but you don't? I hope you will go on trusting Me with your future, because I've got so many amazing things planned for you, girl! You can't see all of the cool places you're going to go and wonderful people you're going to meet, but I can. And trust Me, I have a very active imagination, so you can count on your future being absolutely amazing!

"For the Lord says, 'When seventy years are completed for Babylon, I will visit you and keep My promise to you. I will bring you back to this place. For I know the plans I have for you,' says the Lord, 'plans for well-being and not for trouble, to give you a future and a hope. Then you will call upon Me and come and pray to Me, and I will listen to you. You will look for Me and find Me, when you look for Me with all your heart. I will be found by you,' says the Lord. 'And I will bring you back and gather you from all the nations and all the places where I have made you go,' says the Lord. 'I will bring you back to the place from where I sent you away.'"

JEREMIAH 29:10–14

They Get Away with Everything!

You see those kids who are doing things they shouldn't, and you wonder, "How do they get away with it?" You also wonder, "What would happen if they got caught?" But it seems like they hardly ever get caught. That's so unfair!

Sweet girl, I never promised that life would be fair. I know that's hard to hear, but it's the "unfair things" that will help you grow into an amazing, godly woman.

Take a good look at the seventy-third chapter of Psalms in My book (the Bible). Read the whole chapter from start to finish. David (a king who lived in the olden days) asked Me the very same question you're asking Me now: "Why do the wicked prosper?" He wasn't happy that the bad guys always seemed to get away with stuff. Keep reading the chapter to find out how I answered his question! I whispered a secret truth in David's ear—those ungodly people might have it good now, but it's only temporary. The story won't have a happy ending unless they get their hearts right with Me.

Precious girl, don't worry so much about what's going on with other people—good or bad. Instead of getting so upset over how much better they have it, start thinking about your own story's happy ending. You'll have many years of love, joy, peace, and happiness as you follow Me. They can have that too, if you'll share the message of who I am.

See, this is what the sinful are like. They always have it easy and their riches grow. For no good reason I have kept my heart pure and have not sinned. For I have suffered all day long. I have been punished every morning. I would not have been true to Your children if I had spoken this way. It was too hard for me when I tried to understand this, until I went into the holy place of God. Then I understood their end. For sure, You set the sinful in places where there is danger at every step. You throw them down to be destroyed. How they are destroyed right away! They come to an end with much fear. Like a dream when one wakes up, so You will hate what they look like when You rise up, O Lord.
PSALM 73:12–20

Praise Your Way Through

There are days when you want to stay in bed with the covers pulled up over your head—especially when you're going through tough stuff. But I know you better than that, girl! You hop out of that bed, put a smile on your face, and sing a song of praise to Me. When you do, your courage will rise, rise, rise!

Oh, I know. . .you don't exactly feel like lifting up a song of praise when you're feeling down in the dumps. Who has the time or energy for that? But I'm here to tell you, that's exactly the time you should praise Me the loudest, when you don't feel like it! Praise changes the atmosphere. You can go from doom and gloom to hope and joy with just a few notes of praise! In fact, this is My recipe for overcoming obstacles—praise your way through them. Boy, will you ever feel better! You'll be zapped with courage from on high!

Now, I'm not saying it's going to be easy, but try it and see if I'm right. When you praise Me, all of those things that have been bugging you will fly away, like butterflies on the wind!

Battles will come and go. There's no stopping that. But you know the answer, girl. Praise your way through!

I will honor the Lord at all times. His praise will always be in my mouth. My soul will be proud to tell about the Lord. Let those who suffer hear it and be filled with joy. Give great honor to the Lord with me. Let us praise His name together. I looked for the Lord, and He answered me. And He took away all my fears. They looked to Him and their faces shined with joy. Their faces will never be ashamed. This poor man cried, and the Lord heard him. And He saved him out of all his troubles. The angel of the Lord stays close around those who fear Him, and He takes them out of trouble. O taste and see that the Lord is good. How happy is the man who trusts in Him!

PSALM 34:1–8

More Great Books for Courageous Girls!

100 Extraordinary Stories for Courageous Girls

Girls are world-changers! And this deeply inspiring storybook proves it! This collection of 100 extraordinary stories of women of faith—from the Bible, history, and today—will empower you to know and understand how women have made a difference in the world and how much smaller our faith (and the biblical record) would be without them.

Hardback / 978-1-68322-748-9 / $16.99

Cards of Kindness for Courageous Girls: Shareable Devotions and Inspiration

You will delight in spreading kindness and inspiration wherever you go with these shareable *Cards of Kindness*! Each perforated page features a just-right-sized devotional reading plus a positive life message that will both uplift and inspire your young heart.

Paperback / 978-1-64352-164-0 / $7.99

With your parent's permission, check out **CourageousGirls.com**, where you'll discover additional positive, faith-building activities and resources!

BARBOUR
kidz
A Division of Barbour Publishing